Bert Widman

AF208519

# Ahead Of Their Time

n evolutionary
resentation of
minent heretics.

n plain language.

**Vivant, vivunt !**

**O. A. M. D. G.**

# A C K N O W L E D G E M E N T S

The biographical data of the „heretics", the background of their time and some excerpts from their works were taken with great pleasure and never ending gratitude from Will & Ariel Durant´s „The Story of Civilization", perusing the volumes

| | | |
|---|---|---|
| Cesar And Christ | : | Markion, Origen, Arius, Nestorius |
| The Age Of Faith | : | Emperor Julian |
| The Age Of Reformation | : | Wiclif, Hus, Luther |
| The Age Of Reason Sets In | : | Bruno |
| The Age of Louis XIV. | : | Spinoza |

Consulted for comparison was the publication „2000 Years of Christendom", which appeared 1982 in the publishing house of Andreas & Andreas, Salzburg/Austria.

Profound thanks are extended to the editor and the contributors.

Vilnius, December 20th 1998

Bert Widman

# INTRODUCTION

When Walter and I did our first short book „The Stone Age Of Faith" we sometimes felt the strong temptation to dwell with some extraordinary minds who thought deeply over the revelation through Yeshua but came to results that were rejected by a church which, in its early times, was in dire need of a unified theology, a canon. No guidelines or room for individual thinking, but commanded infallible truth.

From the organization´s point of view it was an act of survival. In the 3rd century there were more than 80 rampant „christian" beliefs, which drew sarcastic comments from the pagan believers.

Today we all know that this early emergency brake was never loosened afterwards. The growing political power of the church influenced emperors and empresses and vice versa so that councils over doctrine were decided mostly by the geo-politics of their time or by the infighting between rival church patriarchates. Very soon it became not enough to denounce dissident believers but to destroy them also physically, to be sure that their thoughts remained dead forever. In this, however, the alliance of throne and altar was very much mistaken indeed.

So one eminent thinker after the other was condemned as a „heretic" (Greek: hairesis = choice). The church saw to it that this neutral term developed a negative slant over the centuries so that it became a notion that spelled spiritiual haugthiness, putting individual thinking or reason above „confirmed truths", a covert or open dismantling of the scriptures and, necessarily so, an attack on the organization even if only articles of faith were questioned.

None of these alleged elements, however, were the driving force of the heretics. Most of them were devout men and committed much more towards a deeper understanding of the message through Yeshua than their orthodox organizations.

When the young church emerged from the political vortex of the crumbling Roman empire as the victor it exercised its power to silence heretics ever more forcibly, with the ever eager help of the „secular arm" which wanted no turmoil on ideological frontiers and had a coveting eye on the wealth of convicted disbelievers.

This attitude, born in the first turbulent centuries, held on over history, compounded by the increasing political and economic power coming to the church organization. The openly heretic became much less in numbers, knowing that the price of their choice was certain death. Many flirted with martyrdom but choose to stay alive. Galilee had many precursors. But still, in practically every century after the turbulent 3rd, 4th and 5th century there were great thinkers who now not only saw some different or new meaning in the revelation through Yeshua but also the widening rift between the faith and an organizsation that turned it into a travesty.

Due to the intended small volume of our first book it was not possible to turn to one of them at length, because if we gave room to one it would have been grossly arbitrary, deeming many others as not so important. So it had to be a new small book dedicated exclusively to eminent „heretics" over the centuries.

Within the necessary selection which we had to face we concentrated on those minds in whom we saw an evolutionary approach to the problems they were wrestling with. Evolutionary in this context means that their reasoning went beyond the grammar of scriptures and over the walls erected by infallible councils, towards a God who was greater than the organization could imagine or allow.

Not only that, however. We invited into our book with preference those minds who felt that our four dimensions and two sexes are ridiculous tools to gauge a reality, person or nature of the Creator. In short, those who showed to their organizations that their so-called God is too small and hopelessly man-imitated.

Lastly, in the combination of all evolutionary directions, those who accorded the reason of the individual more spiritual weight before a Creator than questionable scripts or doctrines of an organization. That is, to see the revelation through Yeshua in free will.

Please listen to our preparatory discussion:

B: It seems that in writing our first book we caught a tiger by the tail. When we started we thought it would be enough to give a „Summa" of our views, the grand scale ...

W: Indeed. What we did not realize at that time is that we had to leave out many decisive details, especially in the „Ballast" part of it. All right, so we wrote the next little volume „Why, Paul ?" But after this was finished we knew that we were not nearly to the end in our search for evolutionary thinking around the revelation. The most promising clue to that were the so-called heretics.

B: How did we arrive at this notion, do you remember?

W: Very well I do. We looked at the present state of the so-called „christian" denominations and found that evolution simply does not occur in them. Of course there are „heretics" in them nowadays also but they do not have the bite or impact of the early dissident thinkers. They have in common that they are unable of or too timid to attack the „big" issues that have been settled for them by councils of old men centuries ago. So they try to doctor the symptoms of a spreading illness instead of going after the bazillus.
Secondly, they prefer to stay „inside" the organization which allows them only a narrow room of maneuvering. They still think that they need an indispensable mother ...

B: He who does not have the church as his mother cannot have God as his father?

W: I would not put it as narrowly as the bishop Cyprian of Carthago formulated this hubris in middle of the 3rd century, no. The reason is that they still believe that their organization is ordained by God; it may be hard to recognize the message through Yeshua in them, but they believe in the possibility of curing the body in time. Outright desertion occurs only to a few who see no remedy any more.

B: I see one more reason why they are having no impact on the believers. All of them suffer from the morbus theologicus, i.e. they speak in a language that is not understood any more by outsiders, laymen, laywomen. They are writing in the infamous tradition of an academic terminology because - that includes the whole clergy, by the way - they desperately want to uphold the impression that their so-called theology is a science; without writing „scientifically" they are afraid not to be taken seriously by the wordly academics. Apparently they never bother to think - those almost-heretics - that radical changes need a radical language especially on the ground level. Above all, an understandable language.

W:  Exactly so. I hold any bet that out of a random sampling of 1.000 catholic believers not one percent have read with understanding the works of Teilhard de Chardin, Kueng or Boff, just to mention a few. And I confess that I had great difficulties with them also.

B:  Was their existence ever jeopardized?

W:  Never physically, of course. Teilhard was silenced by his Jesuit superiors, Popes orders. Kueng lost his chair in the Tuebingen University, which however promptly rallied to him and created a new one for him, ecumenical theology; that was a serious defeat for Mr. Ratzinger, the willing executioner to the Polish Pope.
Boff on the other hand, the Argentine Franciscan, was the only one who finally retaliated openly against the withdrawal of speech and quit priesthood and organization.

B:  500 years ago the church would have loved to put them all on the stake, right?

W:  We are sidetracked now, let´s get down to business. How do we go about our little book?

B:  So we agree that it will be short, no?

W:  Yes, very much so, and in plain language, as the others.

B:  This will leave us with about ten eminent historical persons.

W:  It will be a narrow choice and very much open to criticism because of that ...

B: I am sure that criticism, if any, will be fired on much larger targets of ours, much less on the selection we had to do.

W: That as may be. But I want to propose that we are including into these ten or so personalities also at least one eminent heretic each of the Hebrew and Islamic faith, to show that also they had evolutionary thinkers and that their organization dealt with them in the same infamous way as the „christian" organizations.

B: An interesting idea. Whom do you propose?

W: In the Hebrew faith the choice is quite simple; it can be Spinoza only.

B: I cannot think of a better representative either. And what about Islam?

W: One of their great philosophers in the Middle Ages, a Sufi philosopher perhaps?

B: I am sorry, to this I cannot agree. First of all because philosophers, heretical as their teachings may sound sometimes to orthodox churches, are accorded the freedom of thinking ex definitione. The heretics who are our target group thought and spoke from the inside of their organizations. And what you said about a possible Sufi saint falls short of the goal too, because Sufism in Islam was never banned. Sorry, there we have to look deeper, but I am positive that we shall come across somebody.

W: And if we take a group instead, the Mutazilites of the 9th century?

B: Let us keep this option open if we should not find a clear-cut individual heretic. He has priority, agreed?

W: Fine. And now I propose that in the selection of the rest you are going to nominate half of them and so will I. All right?

B: I like the idea. We have to keep in mind only that the spread of the personalities should span the centuries, not only covering the famous heretics of early „christian theology".

W: So who is your first proposition?

B: I want to nominate Origenes Adamantius, shortly known as Origen, 3rd century, of Alexandria.

W: Why him?

B: Because in my opinion he was the first man of „theological" fame who dared to challenge the litteral, grammatical interpretation of the scripts on Yeshua. In doing so he became the first evolutionary „christian" thinker. Of course he had no concept of evolution as such; the first one to ever introduce this view was Teilhard, in our century. But to say more on Origen would preempt our discussion on him. Agreed?

W: Yes. Along the same line of selection, I nominate Arius. I think that no defence of my choice will be necessary?

B: Certainly not. When I am proposing now Nestor it is because he has touched a decisive issue, where the repercussions are still to be felt today. Our discussion of him will be relatively short because we shall limit ourselves to one outstanding controversial issue only.

W: So be it. It seems that by necessity we have to center on the early centuries. I have no misgivings about it, nor will our readers, because the heretics in these times dealt with far more radical issues than their colleagues of later times; this should not belittle the dedication of those, however.
But taking up the lead from the radical issues I think we owe a discussion to Markion. Don´t you think so?

B: Yes, we felt him very much when we wrote the „Ballast" section of our first book. Agreed.

W: I do not know whether the balance of centuries is becoming too lopsided now if I propose the Emperor Julian, no?

B: Julian Apostata? With him we are still in the 4th century, but I agree that we cannot bypass this great man.

W: The High Middle Ages left little room for open dissent with commanded truths. Too many councils had already constructed too many Prokrustes beds for any proliferating members. Scholastic thinking was acclaimed as a peak achievement of subtle thinking instead of being denounced for what it was, the hubris of mankind to apply terrestrial measuring tools to the Creator. Can you think of an outstanding heretic of this time?

B: Yes, but he was never accused of heresy: Abaelard, between the 12th and 13th century. He was walking a narrow edge and he knew it.

W: Sorry, but this is not quite enough for our purpose. The personalities whom we present must be „authentic" heretics, not only inwardly so.

B: You mean that their views must have been denounced officially by councils or popes?

W: No, they need no dubious quality labels of this sort. Our approach to the minds we want to present is above all the evolutionary aspect of their dissent with orthodox belief. To this we should stick. Undercover heretics simply will not do.

B: As I leaf through the centuries there appears Johannes Hus in my sight. Would he be a fitting choice? At any rate they burnt him. And if we include him, we cannot bypass Wiclif, correct?

W: So much for the word of emperors. Violent death alone, on this we just agreed, is not enough however. We shall look into them whether we see anything evolutionary, all right?

B: It is not because of the burning stake again when I mention Giordano Bruno. His views on God and the universe have been vindicated only recently.

W: I fully agree to him.
But somehow we seem to have forgotten Luther, isn´t it?

B: I was waiting for you to propose him, because I do not.

W: And why not, please?

B: Because for all intents and purposes the organization - his new organization - meant more to him than the plight of peasants or Jews. He started out as a true reformer, agreed. But he ended up like a Pope. I do not see a great contribution from him to the evolution of our consciousness.

W: I beg your pardon, but I do! And with some good will on your side you will agree with me at the end of our discussion. I do not propose, I insist that he will be included!

B: Calm yourself, he is in. Now, how many personalities do we have now, upon first count?

W: Let us see: Markion, Origen, Arius, Nestor, Julian, Wiclif, Hus, Luther and Bruno, that makes 9 from „christian" side and one each from the Jewish and Islamic side, altogether eleven.

B: The temptation is great to raise the number to twelve, no?

W: We should not yield to this; if only to show that numbers are of no importance, but quality of mind.

B: There is one more thing to be agreed upon between us. We have to bring some method into our presentation. I propose that we are going about it this way:

   - First we are giving a concise description of the religious and political ambiente that was prevailing around the person, including the state of the religious organization in which he grew up;

   - Secondly we have to do an assessment of the mental development of the person, looking at his teachers and studies, prevailing doctrines of faith and other governing influences;

   - Thirdly there must be a brief historic account on his major works;

   - Fourthly we present the points of dissident thinking, the struggle with the organization and important critics, culminating in the anathema that is finally thrown at him. Ultimately, his end.

- Number five, and most important to us: how may be he rated under evolutionary aspects and what is his impact still today?

There is no need for a discussion of the first three points. They will be presented in concise narrative form, a digest of the sources we have consulted.

After that our discussion will set in on the points four and five. What do you think of this overall procedure?

W: I seriously doubt that we can live up to this catalog. Expecially with the thinkers in the early centuries we have precious little biographical data, not to speak of the influences surrounding them.

B: Of course we cannot give more than we have. On the other hand I am of the opinion that possible blank spaces in their biography are of secondary importance in our presentation. It is their thoughts, their controversial minds, the impact that they were having and have still today; they are in the foreground.

W: Certainly so. Apparently we have no choice: so some of our contributions will be much shorter than others. This must not be seen as a rating; I am positive that our readers will understand this.

B: Our grip on the tiger´s tail is becoming ever harder. When do we let go?

W: I do not know. Probably never.

# MARKION

## 85 - 150

# THE MAN

When speaking about the roots of Markion we are centering on his spiritual basis, because the biographical data are few and shortly told. He came from the town of Sinope in Asia Minor. Port and town still exist today under the name Sinop on the Southern coast of the Black Sea, Turkey. His year of birth is not reported. Apparently he had inherited a wealthy family business in shipping lines. Whether and how long he managed the enterprise is not mentioned either.

He was a Christian already when he came to Rome around 139/140 and joined the christian community there. Apparently he was very much welcome there, perhaps also owing to the fact that he donated a substantial sum, amount unkown, upon his arrival.

Four years later he was excommunicated and had founded a rival christian church. What happened? In order to explain this we have to make a short excursion into a school of thought by which he had been influenced before coming to Rome, the Gnosis (Greek : knowledge).

Gnosticism existed before Christianity; its message was that the human mind is able indeed to fathom the ideas of God through mystic means. It had produced the concept of a Saviour well before Yeshua was born. The influence of the Gnosis is apparent in the text of the scrolls of Qumran and is to be felt very much in the report of John.

Gnosticism never was organized outwardly; it was inevitable, therefore, that strange notions found their way into the belief which accentuated isolated aspects only instead of erecting a systematic edifice of faith. As an example, Doketism may be cited (Greek : dokein = to seem). The Doketists held that Jesus never had a true human body but vested himself in a „seeming" body only. Small wonder that the young christian church resented this idea because it endangered their concept of redemption, which needed - and still does - the bodily death of Yeshua as the ultimate ransom price payable to an irate deity.

Another cloudy idea of the Gnosis was that in fact there are two Gods. One is the Yahve of the Old Testament who created matter, and matter is evil per se. The God of light and love, therefore, whom Yeshua preached, must be a very different God, who brought the Spirit. In this partitioning of the creation we detect still older notions of Zoroaster.

On the whole the Gnosis was a pessimistic belief. The world is not seen any more as the creation in the biblical sense nor as something fully positive in Plato´s meaning. What remains is the flight out of this evil world, a flight that can be accomplished only in the Spirit.

In one thing, however, the Gnostics fully agreed: The so-called Old Testament of the Hebrew belief, especially their God Yahve, is not the God whom Yeshua preached. The scriptures of this belief do not prepare a fertile but a hostile ground for the revelation through Yeshua. They should be discarded totally, therefore. Small wonder that Paul in his letters repeatedly warns his pupils to steer clear of the Gnosis.

Coming back to Markion: was he a Gnostic? Sometimes he is accorded the title of the greatest Gnostic ever. This is hardly the truth, however, as we shall see.

We are citing Durant first:
„The Christ of the Gospels, said Markion, had described as his father a God of tenderness, forgiveness, and love; but the Yahveh of the Old Testament was a harsh god of unrelenting justice, tyranny, and war; this Yahveh could not be the father of the gentle Christ. What good God, asked Markion, would have condemned all mankind to misery for eating an apple, or desiring knowledge, or loving a woman? Yahveh exists, and is the creator of the world; but he made flesh and bones of man from matter, and therefore left man´s soul imprisoned in an evil frame. To release the soul of man a greater God sent his son to earth, Christ appeared, already thirty years of age, in a phantasmal, unreal body, and by his death won for good men the privilege of a purely spiritual resurrection.

The good, said Markion, are those who renounce Yahveh and the Jewish Law, reject the Hebrew Scriptures, shun marriage and all sensual enjoyment, and overcome the flesh by a stern asceticism.."

We have to thank Will Durant for yet another concise rendition of complicated reasoning.

Markion did not stop halfway, he reasoned further: The highest God, the God of love, is submitting himself out of his own free will to the power of Yahveh in an exchange for the souls of mankind. It may be noted that Origen later on gave a variation of the theme. With him it was not Yahveh who was tricked in the deal, but the sheitan was outmaneuvered because he could not hold power anymore over mankind.

Good is now everything which is not of this world, ascetism and martyrdom in the first line. Evil is all that ties man to this world. Markion bows out graciously from the final reckoning: the new God will not hold a final judgement, the worthy soul enters into the new God. But then Markion is carried away by intolerance in saying that the non-believers will find no mercy with the new God; instead they remain in the hand of Yahveh who indeed will subject them to judgement.

Consequently, Markion now developed a canon of his belief: The Old Testament is not a scripture of revelation, it refers to Yahveh and has to stay outside of the christian belief completely, therefore.

Rigorously he also demanded that the New Testament must be cleaned of any connections to Judaic law and Hebrew belief, which, in his opinion, have poisoned the revelation through Yeshua.

The most astonishing feature in his canon is the fact, however, that he rates Paul to be the most exact renditioner of Yeshua´s teachings. Somehow he must have overlooked Paul´s letter to the Hebrews. Besides him and the report of Luke he cancels out every other scripture and is even the editor of Luke, striking out the infancy tales on Yeshua and his pedigree, practically almost everything from the first two chapters and much of the third. In contrast to the Gnosis Markion accepts history but wants to see it purified.

He conceded to christianism that it is a religion of redemption, but twists the redemption into his scenario where Christ does not redeem man from trespasses but pulls him out of a misery which is attributable to Yahveh only. And, for good measure, he brings in the Doketist idea that Christ did not die nor was he resurrected because he never had a human body.

There are no „Works" of Markion that have come upon us as a sum of his teachings. He was more a man of action, so we have to look at his doings.

When the christian community could not bear any more with his ideas it excommunicated him. The donation which he made upon his entry was returned to him, which may be seen as either as an act of fairness or of a superstition that if not blood, but certainly high treason clung to the coins.

His followers, however, were numerous. With them Markion founded an own church organization, and he was an able organizer. Within a short short time his creed boasted its own church buildings, presbyters, bishops - and martyrs. It became a serious rival to the orthodox church and spread its belief with missionary zeal. Only around the beginning of the fourth century it gradually lost its influence - 150 years after his uprising.

# THE DISCUSSION

B:  What contribution to the evolution of reason do we owe to
    Markion?

W:  In order to ascertain that we best follow the method of
    elimination i.e. that we deduct those concepts which we feel are
    definitely n o t  evolutionary. Agreed? Then let us start:

    The gnostic view of two competing gods may have sounded
    logical at his time. The belief in one Creator as revealed by the
    Logos through Yeshua, however, makes far more evolutionary
    sense. Markion could not reconcile the evil in the world with
    one Creator, because in his reasoning then also the evil was
    created - or admitted - by him. Instead of looking to the origin of
    evil in the mind of man - which is free will, mind you - he
    charged its origin to Yahve and found the manifestation of evil
    in matter of any form. Man is imprisoned by matter because
    matter produces the desires of this world. We are recognizing
    in this posture the ideas of Buddha and later Hindu
    philosophers but do not know whether this influence really
    existed or if it was parallel thinking by Markion.

B:  We have given our answer to that in the section „How evil is
    evil?" in our first book. There is nothing to be added; so
    Markion is not scoring a point here. I continue:

    The Doketist notion of an ethereal body of the Christ does not
    hold water either, simply because it was not necessary. Yeshua
    was human and of human origin; the Logos used him, to put it
    bluntly, but certainly not against his free will. It cannot be
    repeated often enough that the Logos did not commandeer his
    mind incessantly, but only when he felt it necessary he dictated
    to Yeshua what to speak. „I am not speaking from myself, but
    how I hear I speak," remember? When the voice from within
    was silent, Yeshua spoke and acted on his own in all daily
    affairs, he got hungry, thirsty and human mortal fear crept into
    him before the Temple Guard caught up with him. So, let´s
    discard the notion of an ethereal body.

W: Non-evolutionary was also his intolerance towards non-believers, but I think it was common with all creeds of his time to hurl anathemas at each other, something which the pagan philosopher Celsus found as ridiculous as later on Emperor Julian.

But after having eliminated these notions we come now to the outstanding evolutionary thought of Markion: that the so-called Old Testament together with the oral tradition drawn from it is not the necessary prerequisite for the revelation through Yeshua. He never used the word „tribal history" but gave it revelation character also, a revelation of the „bad" God Yahve, however. To this, of course, we do not subscribe.

The fact, however, that Hebrew faith and Judaic law that originate from the so-called Old Testament are incompatible with the Creator whom Yeshua preached held true then and does so today.

B: I am always a little wary when you use the words „true" or „false". This rings of dogmatic intransigence; the questionable tool of the anathema is never very far from it.

W: I am sorry, but expressions like „high probability" are not of any value in this discussion. Would it satisfy you if I said „true/false in our opinion?"

B: I like this very much indeed. Please proceed!

W: The difficulty we have in the exclusion of the so-called Old Testament from the revelation through Yeshua is the fact that Yeshua himself connected to it very much, pointing to the scriptures that, he told them, advertised the appearance of the Logos. The whole speech, parables and arguments of Yeshua are inextricably tied to the Hebrew canon.

B: How else should it have been? Most of the Jewish listeners did not understand him even when he stressed this connection. Had the Logos told him to waive it and to preach a cosmically interested God then even the precious few who accepted the message would have walked away from him.

W: We also have to remember that the Logos said through him that he had been sent to the children of Israel in the first line and that salvation is to come through the Jews, no?

B: Yes, on the other hand you have to think of the fact that the most intense and unconditional belief in him came from non-Jewish persons, who begged him for the life of a sick child or slave, for instance. Such belief he had not found in Israel, commented the Logos through him.

W: So the Logos changed his mind, considered the Jews as a lost cause and finally appointed Paul to bring the revelation to the pagans?

B: If we can agree that the Logos, whom we do not consider to be omniscient, has indeed changed his mind upon these experiences, you are right in my opinion.

W: If you read the letter of Paul to the Hebrews you are not gaining the idea that he tried to disconnect the revelation from the Old Testament, nor from their law and faith. On the contrary, he is using every possible argument to strengthen these ties, to accord them the basic character without which the teachings of Yeshua the Christ could not be understood. And finally we hear the Logos from Yeshua saying that he had not come to dissolve the law, but to bring it to fulfillment. This, and the warning not to change one iota of the law - how do you reconcile all this against the grand abolition of the so-called Old Testament?

B: For several reasons. First, because of its man-inspired idea of a God, to whom more human behaviour than is digestible had been attributed. Secondly, because of the elitist notion that Israel was a „chosen people". Thirdly, because there never was any evolution in the Hebrew faith, not then, not nowadays. Point four: the Logos really changed his mind, as you said. And the salvation will be taken from the Jews and given to the pagans, remember that also?

W: If the Logos really rated the Jews as a lost cause, then why Yeshua had to die?

B: We have answered this, too, in our first book, but let us repeat it here. Yeshua was very much a Jew and saw his messianic role tied to the sinister prophecies of his people. He wanted to die in fulfillment thereof.

W: Could not the Logos have talked him out of it, showing him the futility of the effort?

B: Maybe he tried to, maybe not, because also Yeshua had his free will and this was set on the old salvation formula for his people.

W: This is the only explanation that is open to me also. But coming back now to Markion: is it justified to discard the so-called Old Testament or not?

B: Not for what it really is, a rich account of tribal history. But as a commanded tenet of faith, incorporated without exception into the revelation from Yeshua, or being the indispensable basis thereof - no. In that Markion took a big evolutionary step forward.

With the increasing secular power of the orthodox church he was declared anathema. How much of this ban was attributable to the gnostic or Doketist elements in his teaching, and how much to his demand to eliminate the so-called Old Testament from the christian faith, this we shall never know. His teachings were condemned as a whole.

W: How do we leave Markion here?

B: He was an uncompromising mind. His case is another proof of the sad fact that the young church stood to gain many evolutionary steps by men like him, but chose precarious unity at the cost thereof. And this applies up to our days.

# ORIGEN

**185 - 254**

# THE MAN

Origenes Adamantius, as his full name was, grew up in Alexandria, a town that looked back on a rich tradition since Alexander The Great founded it in 332 B.C.. Famous for its ideally situated merchant port the town attracted trade and crafts and soon became the hub of the exports from Egypt to the Mediterranean world. At all times, market crossroads were also the ideal exchanges for gossip, tales, philosophy, superstitions and religions.

Philosophy and the arts need a certain amount of luxury. With the first there is no use in preaching to empty bellies; for the second, it needs buyers. Well before Origen was born in 185 A.C. the town had provided a wealthy ambiente for both.

The ethnic cauldron of Alexandria had also a large Hebrew community whose ancestors or members had fled Palestine when the Roman empire crushed the Hebrew uprisings in the first and second century. It can safely be assumed that it was a wealthy community. By the crossroad function of Alexandria, however, the Hebrews were exposed increasingly to the influence of the Greek philosophers and also to gnostic ideas.

When christianity reached Alexandria, therefore, it found already a vivid interchange of judaic theology and hellenistic philosophy, especially so with the stoic-platonic ideas. Educated paganism had long since subscribed to Platon and Aristoteles; in its pantheon was always room enough for new Gods and be it the genius of the present Roman emperor.

We know little on the development of the christian faith in Alexandria until the middle of the second century. At that time, however, existed already one of the first catechetical schools. As the head of this institution, Clemens of Alexandria steps into history.

In order to have spiritual access to Origen´s ideas we have to stay a little with his teacher Clemens. He was born between 140 and 150 and died around 215.

His theology drew important elements from Greek philosophy already. How is it, he asked, that God who is beyond matter reveals himself to man, guiding him in His providence instead of simply leaving him to his destiny? His answer: God wants to educate man. This Educator is the Logos (Greek: word, sense) who not only existed before the creation of this world but has been also shaping the history of mankind. By him God educates man to ever greater insight, accumulating from one generation to the next.

Then the Logos became man. Clemens saw this as a decisive, if not final plateau of education, Christ reveals the full insight into God. By undergoing baptism man becomes part of the spiritual connection to the Logos and God. Only now, says Clemens, the ethical progress of mankind can begin, not because of its own striving but by the gift of God, the Logos.

In retrospect we see the seeds of future controversy already, of course. First of all, Clemens saw Yeshua the man and the Logos as an entity, the Christ. The Logos became man by slipping into the „flesh" as one would don a robe. Clemens does not bother long with the question whether this Christ also was truly a human being, he could not foresee that the discussion of this point should become a disruptive momentum over the next centuries. For him Christ was the Divine Pedagogue and all other details he considered to be irrelevant in comparison.

A good portion of his views is evidently gnostic, i.e. the dualism between matter and spirit. But for him matter is not evil in itself but more so a barrier to the human mind who struggles to find a way through and above it into the superseding spiritual layer of the creation.

Platon had done remarkably well already by putting the idea or concept of a thing above the thing itself. The Logos, in Clemens opinion, now worked a twofold kingsway into the human mind: matter is a kaleidoscope of passing shapes, as Plotin formulated it a century later, the ideas are the formative power. Secondly: through the Logos mankind gains access to the ideas of God through which all matter in the universe has come into being.

Unfortunately also a certain elitist view crept into the thinking of Clemens which should have the due negative effects in later centuries and up to our times. According to him the church is the community of those who more or less grasp the inside of this revelation, an insight provided by God, however, not by human reason. For him these are the real christians, the rest are nominal members only. The real christians form the life of the church.

Those who have been granted more insight than others are to be the officials of the church, its spokesmen. The more insight, the greater the responsibility entrusted to them. The temptation for us nowadays to comment on a reverse possibility is almost irresistible.

This was the ambiente into which Origen was born. His parents were devout christians and he was one of the most attentive listeners whom Clemens had in his catechetical school.

But fate struck rapidly. When he was seventeen (202) the emperor Septimius had decided on yet another persecution of christians in the empire. Origen´s father, whose profession we do not know, was arrested, stood his ground and was condemned to death. In the young man erupted a wild desire to share his fate; the mother, a very sensible woman apparently, hid his clothes so that he could not step outside the house. So Origen could only send the famous message to his father: „Beware not to change your mind on our account!" The father, being a Roman citizen, was beheaded and the task to care for the mother and six younger children fell on Origen.

We do not know how well he shouldered the task of supporting his family. Not too well probably, if we see his increasing spiritual involvement into christian principles parallel to the blood-spilling terror around him. We may console ourselves however by the fact that the christian community always showed its finest strains during a persecution; in doubt his family will have received the necessary support from other church members.

„Increasing spiritual involvement" may not describe adequately Origen´s state of mind in these days. As any young man of his age he was prone to the excesses of a fiery belief, so he adopted ascetic life. Little sleep, much fasting, no shoes, no bed. It can only be related to this pious exaltation that he castrated himself.

There is no indication further on that he came to regret this deed which the Logos through Yeshua considered to be an understandable and commendable step of the will to free itself from the desires of this world. Gibbon has summed up our opinion: „As it was Origen´s general practice to allegorize Scripture it seems unfortunate that, in this instance only, he should have adopted the litteral sense."

In 203 Origen succeeded Clemens as the head of the catechetical school. Inspite of his youth he drew not only christians but also pagan students who spread his teachings and fame in the Mediterranean world.

We are jumping his works here, which will be presented in the following later.

Demetrius, then bishop of Alexandria, looked at the young celebrity with a jaundiced eye. When Origen wanted to join the priesthood he denied it on the grounds that his castrate status would be incompatible with it; either Demetrius had not looked into the report from Matthew for a long time or he simply used this pretext to eliminate competition early enough.

Undeterred by that Origen won his ordination from two Palestinian bishops who consecrated him in 231, whereupon Demetrius promptly excommunicated him.

Origen migrated to Caesarea and founded his own catechetical school there, continuing his prolific writing which was the awe and delight of his contemporaries.

Emperor Decius unleashed another persecution of the christians, in 250 the wave struck also Caesarea. Origen was imprisoned and tortured in best inquisition style but managed to survive until death came to Decius in 251. Upon his release not his mind was broken, but his body, which never recovered from the torture inflicted on him. He continued to live for three years more but succumbed finally in 254, unbending, poor as ever, and famous. We do not know his grave.

At that time philosophy had come to a point where it did not trust the senses any more to bring more insight into the man-world - God relation. Instead it turned to the invisible realm, producing the Neo-Pythagoreans and Neo-Platonists who established mystic theosophy.

Since the Christian belief was spreading rapidly it was almost inevitable that some philosophers, Christian and pagans alike, tried to find a unified theory that would bring Plato´s ideas and Yeshua´s teaching together. Two eminent thinkers have to be mentioned of this era, who exerted early influence also on Origen, Ammonius Saccas and his student Plotinus. We must look at Plotinus a little closer in order to follow the spiritual development of Origen.

His written legacy consisted of a compilation of doctrinal essays into which his later editor Porphyry brought some structure, arranging them in groups of nine each; because of this number the total work was called the Enneads.

In contrast to the Gnosis Plotinus did not consider matter as evil. Matter, he said, is only the formless possibility of form. He conceded to matter a hidden energy, or soul, whenever it takes form. (There is no big step, in hindsight, to think of the concept of self-organization of matter in today´s physics). Only, in retrospect again, he reversed evolution by maintaining that the lower reality cannot produce the higher; it is the higher being, the soul, that produces the lower form. So is the human body formed in time by the desires of the soul.

He believed like the Hindus in a migration of the soul; each new corporeal existence is the result of virtues or vices in the preceding form until it will melt some day into the light of the Creator.

For the survival of the personality he saw no necessity; the soul is energy which returns to and dissolves in the limitless life-giving principle that pervades the universe.

Origen and Plotinus were fellow pupils and became friends for life, the pagan philosopher opening the grand view of the matter-forming universal energy that we see e.g. in nature (to which Spinoza would find some 1400 years later), the christian philosopher left with the worrisome task of interweaving this vista with 2000 years of Hebrew doctrine and the 200 years since the revelation through Yeshua. It was quite evident that the results would please the pagans much more than the orthodox church.

Some contemporaries of Origen estimated the total number of his books, brochures, comments to be around 6.000. While this figure might be taken with several grains of salt because of oriental hyperbole there remains no doubt that he was the most widely read, respected and influential christian writer of his era.

We are picking out only a few outstanding works here. As the first one the „Hexapla" (Greek: sixfold) which was an overdue correction of the Septuaginta in a parallel collated presentation of the Hebrew text of the Old Testament, his own translation into the Greek language and, for comparison, the translation of the Septuaginta. It was the first recorded event of semantic comparison of scriptures. The work required two decades and a task force of enduring copyists whom he probably found among his students.

Knowing by heart the four reports on Yeshua since boyhood times he wrote commentaries not only on these but on every book in the Bible.

In his „Peri archon" - First Principles - he produced the first methodical principles of the christian faith. The work „Stromateis" - Miscellany - in which Origen tried to bolster christian tenets of faith by basically concurring opinions of pagan writers, the Greek philosophers in the first line, demonstrates his arrow of thinking already very clearly.

As publisher of the Hexapla Origen concentrated on the best possible translation of the Septuaginta, word for word. It is astounding that this work, which allegedly took two decades to finish, should not leave him with a firm and exclusive belief in anything else but a litteral interpretation of the texts. Quite to the contrary. Probably because he saw what havoc translators can work on texts which are sometimes ambiguous within themselves, and probably because he fixed his gaze into the distant future where he saw legions of translators at work he began to have doubts not only in the letter but also in the spirit of many verbatim tenets of faith.

He came to the opinion that a litteral meaning of the texts clouds the view to a more fundamental spiritual insight which could be reached by an allegoric interpretation only. Following that he did away with the litteral account of the Genesis, with the man-inspired deals that a Jahve handed to Israel, the legend of a Garden Eden and even with certain stories from the reports on Yeshua, e.g. his temptation by the Sheitan.

The formula he found is not only valid for „christian" belief, but in our opinion also for Islam: sometimes scriptural stories were invented to underline a basic truth. Who adheres to the letter invariably gets  confronted with reason which then, of course, is of the devil, in orthodox opinion.

His most daring statement on the scriptures was that they contain basic truth only. New insights could lead as well to different answers as the Apostles had given. In our opinion this was addressed foremost to Paul, but we have no proof thereof.

In order to be short we present the further highlights of this daring mind in pointer words only:

- The Logos is God´s ideas of the world; therefore the Logos is the instrument of creation and the interpreter of God´s ideas;

- The Logos proceeding from God is of one being with him, but subordinate to him;

- Redemption is not a release of bondage from sin but a spiritual grace that opens the view to a transcendent life;

- The incarnation of the Logos in Yeshua and the dispute of the resulting „physis" is of small importance compared to the revelation coming through Yeshua;

- The Logos appeared as a doctor and teacher to this world. The death of Yeshua is only an example for accepting suffering in good countenance;

- The devil (in which Origen believed) has been cheated by the revelation through Yeshua, because before that man was the prey of the devil simply by not having enough insight;

- The soul departing from the human body will have to pass through a succession of purification stages before being allowed in God´s presence. In the end, however, all souls will be saved. In that he put the revelation in sharp contrast to Plotinus´ concept. For Origen there was never any doubt that the soul, inspite of prior migrations, would preserve its individuality in the final dimension.

- This world will end in fire, but there will be another material world after, and after. Each world will be an improved design and the whole sequence is the manifestation of the designs and ideas of God.

By allowing allegorical interpretation and individual judgement of the scriptures, especially so of the four reports on Yeshua, Origen knew that he was on a collision course with the orthodox church. His system allowed manifold „theologians" after him to use it as a quarry from which they could mine building materials for their views - for or against him. What followed was an atomisation of the edifice of thought which Origen had erected and an arbitrary emphasis given to some elements thereof. All this heated the discussion within the church and was - in the end - also responsible for the grand dogmatic fights of the third and fourth century.

Still, the church took a long time to condemn him. This is understandable because in the preceding fights of the factions each side could - and did - draw munition from Origen. Finally, in the year 400, quite some time after the council of Nicaea, Pope Anastasius declared his opinions as blasphemous. It was left to the council of Constantinople 553 to throw the final anathema at him - only now he was a heretic.

As Durant sums it up: with him christianity ceased to be only a comforting faith; it became a full-fledged philosophy, buttressed by Scripture but proudly resting on reason.

# THE DISCUSSION

W: The first thought which comes into my mind when considering the life, work and thoughts of Origen is that all is of one cast. His life carried his works and his works carried the life. There is no ambiguity in between them. I am saying this because we have looked at so many philosophers, especially at those from the 18th century onward, and saw a lot of ambiguity between their private lives and their lofty pronouncements. Character and teachings were sometimes worlds apart.

B: My dear friend, this reeks very much of Donatism. Donatus in the 4th century was a purist. He was of the debatable opinion that a sinful priest could not effectively transport the sacraments to a believer. The young church could not tolerate the idea because it would have opened the inquest into each priest´s conduct by the community, which then was to be the final arbiter of really working sacraments. Very justifiedly so, Donatus was silenced. So it is with the philosophers; if we would put the standard of Origen to them precious few would qualify. Just think of Rousseau who gave away his children to foundling homes.

W: This is the major reason why I think of him as an empty vessel only. Very conveniently rattling when you knock against it - but empty.

B: Coming back to Origen, his vessel was full to the brim. We are discussing his evolutionary aspects. What we consider to be evolutionary we have laid down in our introduction. Now what?

W: I think his major evolutionary achievement was that he dared to look at the Scriptures not in the litteral way but to put allegorical interpretation and increased human reason into the foreground, above words and grammar.

B: If you say increased, just what do you mean?

W: He looked at his times and he looked to the horizon. At his times, he saw not only the possibility but the compulsion to tie Platonic ideas to the revelation through Yeshua. The Logos as the sum of ideas which God has upon the world - or creation as whole - is very much consistent with the revelations.

Looking to the horizon, he became very evolutionary by maintaining that any increment accorded to the human power of reason will open up new vistas to the same revelation.

In other words: the revelation is not a square monolith that anchores certain truths unchangeable forever but is a yeast put into the fertile mind of a population that has the power of reflexive thinking and free will. In that it will ferment the thinking incessantly towards a greater God.

B: So be it. Now it is my turn: I think that Origen was on purpose ambigous on the co-habitation of the Logos in Yeshua the man, something that later councils threw in the waste basket of belief, namely that the Spirit communicating through Yeshua to us was an entity in itself and did not mix with the human nature of this venerable man. He did not say so expressly, however.

W: Why should Origen have adopted this nebulous attitude?

B: Because it did not mean very much to him. He concentrated on the bigger issue. For him it was not necessary, futile even, to put the scalpel of limited human reason to events that were - and are - forever outside of our grasp. It is a great pity that the Scholastic thinkers forgot this truth.

W: Let us stay there for a minute, please. What you are saying means that the mind of Yeshua was commandeered by the Logos?

B: Very much so, and certainly not against but with the full consent of this man. He had offered himself to become a tool, and he became a magnificent one.

W: Apparently so, but certainly not in one run throughout the few years on which we have the four reports. When we read them we see the eternal Logos talking from him but we also see Yeshua undergoing in his human mind and physique the tribulations which befall all of us.

B: Certainly.He openly declared that - when the Logos was taking over in dialectic situations - that he speaks as he hears. So he was the echo of the Logos. What we do not understand today is that Yeshua presented himself to his listeners at all times as an entity. He, in his flesh, was the „Son of God" an not only the carrier of the Logos. Small wonder that the Israelites wanted to stone him when he told them that he existed before Abraham.

W: Origen put one more criterion on the Logos: he is subordinate to God.

B: One of the astounding things is that this difference, which the Logos in Yeshua repeated many times, was not upheld by the evolving faith. We shall have more on this when we are discussing Arius. A few items, however, are in place here already.

W: Such as?

B: For one the Logos did not bring the revelation to this planet by his own will. He was sent - ordered to in our understanding - to do so. This he repeated a hundred times probably. Secondly, he did not like the population to which he was sent. He often decried it as those feeble in mind, as the obstinate and despisable lot that only ment to have a God but had only a deity. Thirdly, he openly declared that he was not omniscient.

W: And Origen, did he recognize these contradictions?

B: He must have. Otherwise his theory of subordination makes no sense.

W: Stepping around the issue: do we rate the revelation through Yeshua any less because the Logos is subordinate to God?

B: Origen thought about this also and his answer is the same as we are giving today: not in the least. Through the Logos speaking from Yeshua we know that the Creator of this universe, right through the immensity of time, space, galaxies and solar systems will recognize beings of free will. Very personably so, you, me, every personality of this planet and of all other habitats in the universe where reflexive thinking has sprouted. I am basking in this incredible view which has been made credible by the revelation through Yeshua and I thank the Divine Power morning, day and night for this immeasurable grace. What is it to me, therefore, not to understand the intricate relationship between the Logos and God? Origen must have thought on the same lines.

W: This is the way I feel too. What a disgrace on the other hand, seeing congregations of old men wrestling with each other in the decades and centuries after Origen to establish the rank or nature of a Father, a Son and of a Spirit. I rate it simply as human hyperbole where the amoeba tries to develop a grid system into which her ambiente must fit by necessity.

B: Not a bad comparison. Coming back to Origen, however, we have to acknowledge that some of his opinions were certainly not so evolutionary. I think of his teaching - which was apparently influenced by Paul - that the insane slaughtering of the man Yeshua, the Logos-carrier, was the redemption prize to be paid to God in order to reconciliate him with mankind again. In my opinion this is clearly stone-age reasoning.

W: He was much more subtle than your dictum. Since he believed in the Sheitan as a very personal anti-force to God, giving him combatant status, he saw the driving force in the devil to keep the developing reflexive minds in despondency, ignorance and sin. The Sheitan had no hold on Yeshua, however. Origen was mingling Yeshua and the Logos together into „Christ", certainly, something to which we object again. But having no hold on Christ, he says, the Sheitan was tricked out of his plan. For all future, Origen says, Yeshua´s untouchability was the devil´s undoing. For all followers of Christ - or of the revelation in our language - became untouchable to him. The freeing of reason, casting away the shackles of ignorance and despondency, was triumphantly on the march. Seen that way the life and death of Yeshua was a watershed indeed, but not a prize to be paid to an irate deity.

B:  I have to come back once more to the problem we are having with Yeshua´s attitude, making no difference to the outside between his human origin and status and of God´s Spirit that not only rested on him but told him exactly what to say, verbatim, and Yeshua confirmed that he only repeated to the outside what he first heard inside him. And still he called himself „Son of God", physique and all, which was taken not only as as provocation by his fellow Hebrews but as a blasphemy. Why did he not confine himself to say: God is speaking through me. Are you having any explanation for that?

W:  None at all. He was not carried away by the fact that he had been singled out as the instrument of communication to this world, so it certainly was not delusion of grandeur. The only reason I could see is that the Logos in him was very much embittered with the species he had to come to, as we are hearing him several times. He might have told Yeshua: „This species is deaf to my message anyway. Do not bother to explain my Being in you, therefore, because they cannot or will not understand nor believe it. Call yourself „Son of God" because I have made you that before the Divine Power. You know that they will kill your body because they cannot suffer what I am telling them through you. A blasphemy in their opinion will only hasten this inevitable process. So let it be, Son of God!"

B:  I am not satisfied at all with this idea but there is hardly any room for guesswork. What I fail to understand, however, is the apparent fact that when they were nailing Yeshua´s limbs to the cross the Logos left him. „God, my God, why have you relinquished me?" These words were not sighed, but roared in an ultimate outburst of utter desperation, as we read. And don´t come now with the Stone Age explanation of the „christian" churches that God wanted him to die in despair as the unsurpassable sacrifice for our redemption! What happened really?

W: I am inviting Origen to give us the answer: turn your gaze and mind on the message through Yeshua instead of trying to probe God´s mind. It is far more important to create a breakthrough for the revelation on this planet than trying to apply human logic to events that are forever closed to us as long as we are in our body. Concentrate on the essential. Spread the message, peacefully. Make the world a habitat of people who respect and tolerate each other, in whatever way they may speak to the Divine Power that has been revealed to us. Yeshua´s Sermon on the Mount is the essence, not his death.

B: Well spoken. It sounded very much „live" and encouraging. How are we going to close the chapter on Origen?

W: 1700 years of a progressive build-up of reason have proven him right. We have indeed come to different answers than some Apostles, and especially in contrast to Paul, as Origen had predicted it. A progress that certainly had a high price, to be paid in blood and tears. If we move confidently to new horizons and shedding ballast on the way we see Origen not behind, but always in front of us. The word „evolution" did not exist for him. Instead, he lived it.

B: What would be a fitting epitaph for him?

W: TE QUAERENS CONSUMOR - in search of you I am wasting myself.

# ARIUS

## ? - 337

# THE MAN

Arius had never intended to throw an incendiary into the church nor, least of all, into the empire. However, it became nothing short of such drama.

It is fitting therefore perhaps, that we should shortly present the „dramatis personae" that enacted the spectacle before the pagan population which was quite amused at first before recognizing that the final act, in whatever outcome, was spelling their doom.

There is Arius who pointed out obvious inconsistencies in the Father-Son relations in the christian faith.

There is his bishop Alexander, later on his successor Athanasius, who viewed his teachings as heretic and battled him to the end.

Waiting in both sides of the wings are the followers of Origen. He had preempted the basic ideas of Arius already but in the way of the „Sic et non" - yes and no - as Abaelard would bring it to perfection 900 years later.

The center stage at all times in the drama is commanded by the emperors, Constantine in the first line, who saw the christian faith and its hierarchical organization as the indispensable unifying factor of the empire.

Against the backdrop we see the chorus of bishops of the Eastern church, Origenists in their majority, who were content with the ambiguity of their philosopher and had no taste for the radical Yes or No which Arius demanded.

Invisible on the stage but always well represented by proxies are the Roman popes who watched with increasing concern how the Eastern church was wrestling free from their primate and theological preponderance.

There are many other protagonists whose influence was felt in every act. To do justice to them, however, would have inflated this chapter in an undue way. The interested reader is invited to turn to the rich literature on the subject. Conciseness means concentrating on the essentials by necessity; the price to be paid is the omission of colourful and interesting detail. It is impossible to have it both ways, alas.

And now, after this short prologue, the action may unfold.

Unfortunately we do not know anything about the roots of Arius and precious little about the man. He was a christian who had been ordained to priesthood in Alexandria and served as presbyter at the Baucalis church in the town. It is thought that he came from Baucalis, a town in Northern Egypt. When and why he moved to Alexandria is not known. His contemporary Plotinus has given us an impression of the man in his „Enneads":

„He was tall and thin, of melancholy look, and an aspect that showed traces of his austerities. He was known to be an ascetic, as could be seen from his costume - a short tunic without sleeves, under a scarf that served as a cloak. His manner of speaking was gentle; his addresses were persuasive. The consecrated virgins, who were numerous in Alexandria, held him in great esteem; and he counted many staunch supporters among the higher clergy."

Poring over the scriptures, especially over the four reports on Yeshua , we may safely assume that he was struck with the admissions of Yeshua where he professed that he could not work out of himself, that he said as he heard within him first and that he was not omniscient.

Arius came to important conclusions. For one, that the Logos, the „Son", could not be co-eternal with the „Father" because he had been „begotten" and that meant in time. If the biological notion of birth is discarded however and the Logos was created, then he was made as the whole creation from nothing (ex nihilo) and not from the „Father's" substance, a lesser God therefore. Lastly, the Holy Spirit emanates from the Logos and is even less God than the „Son", therefore.

Had Arius followed the cautios Origen in cloaking his ideas in questions or double-exit formulations the orthodox church would have viewed him as an eccentric theologian only that had to be monitored carefully, of course. Arius was cut from different wood. He went public with his ideas without any philosophical camouflage. This was tantamount to declaration of war to the foundations of the system and bishop Alexander promptly recognized the disruptive element. A closed-door session with the rebel priest was a foregone instrument since Arius had already gathered a strong following in the higher clergy, so only surgery would do. Alexander called a council of Egyptian bishops which, upon his insistence, defrocked Arius and his fellow priests and denounced his teachings. The acts of the trial were then distributed to bishops in the East - with unexpected results, however.

Quite a few bishops were of the opinion that Arius hat not received a fair trial. This undecided attitude fanned the sparks into wildfire; the followers of Arius, priests and laymen alike, realized that the church leaders were divided over the issue and started a missionary activity that in a short time polarized practically every christian city in Northern Africa and in the Asian provinces. The fight of ideas very soon became a fight of fists in the streets, viewed with undisguised pleasure by the pagan citizens.

The noise could not fail to reach emperor Constantine who thereupon sent both Alexander and Arius a personal letter that has been passed on to posterity by Eusebius, a letter that showed how grossly Constantine (and 1200 years later Charles V.) underrated the „Mönchs-Gezänk", German for a heated dispute among monks.

Constantine´s prime concern was to uphold the empire, not theology. We quote him from Eusebius:

„I had proposed to lead back to a single form the ideas which all people conceive of the Deity; for I feel strongly that if I could induce men to unite on the subject, the conduct of public affairs would be considerably eased. *) But alas! I hear that there are more disputes among you than recently in Africa. The cause seems to be quite trifling, and unworthy of such fierce contests. You, Alexander, wished to know what your priests were thinking on a point of law, even on a portion only of a question which in itself is entirely devoid of importance. And you, Arius, if you had such thoughts, should have kept silence ... There was no need to make these questions public ... since they are problems that only idleness raises, and whose only use is to sharpen men´s wits ... these are silly actions worthy of inexperienced children and not of priests or reasonable man ..."

---

*) This candid admission was not repeated by Constantine ever after.

Constantine failed to recognize the importance of an iota. The Greek „homousia" meant „of one substance", Father and Son. Arius however proclaimed „homoiousia", similar being only, expressing the lesser standing of the Logos. The church was acutely aware of the explosive quality of this one letter. The fight was going on inspite or because of the ineptitude of Constantine's letter. The emperor was jolted out of his complacency, however, when he realized that the only tie which politically stabilized his realm, the christian church, was in danger of splitting, something he could not tolerate. This is why he called all bishops to meet in an universal council in Nicaea, Bithynia, in 325. It was attended by 318 bishops, most of them from the Eastern provinces. Pope Silvester I. could not participate because of an illness and was represented by clerics of his Roman court, and - not officially of course - by Constantine's court bishop, Hosius.

A compliment must be paid to the endurance of Constantine, who presided over the meetings, listened patiently to the debates, moderated the violence of the debating parties and engaged himself into arguments also.

Bishop Alexander was accompanied by his archdeacon Athanasius who proved to be the most formidable adversary to Arius. He maintained that if the Logos and the Holy Spirit were not of one substance with the Father the christian faith would end in polytheism, so reason must bow to mystery. To the end, only seventeen bishops sided with Arius, perhaps not so much because of Athanasius' arguments but seeing rival churches springing up in their dioceses and losing their grip on power, therefore.

So the council struck the iota out and confirmed the belief „... in Jesus Christ, the Son of God, begotten, not made, being of one essence (homousios) with the Father ...".

There is no evidence that Constantine rigorously pressed for this result because we may assume that inwardly he despised the theological dogfight now as before. But he had to preserve unity.

Had the majority voted otherwise he probably would have been content as well. His court bishop Hosius of Cordoba, however, his theological adviser, clearly sided with Rome. Since Tertullian the formula of the Western church was „unius substantiae", that is „homousios". Probably yielding to his influence Constantine proposed that this adjective be accepted.

Only Arius and two bishops refused to sign the document, to the triumph of Athanasius and to the immense relief of the emperor. Feeling safe again now, Constantine added the punishment of exile to the three heretics, ordered the burning of Arius´books and made possession of them a capital crime. For him the matter was closed.

In fact it remained wide open because Arius had too many followers already that were not to be muzzled by the council or the emperor. The discussion was kept aflame especially in the East, fanned not only by the Arians but also by Non-Arians, the faction called „Origenists", who felt that the term „homousios" was too vague a notion that would breed further conflict.

Constantine was monitoring the development closely and had to admit that his prime concern, to preserve the unity of the church and with it, that of the imperium, was not put to rest by the council; on the contrary. In order to ease the tensions he decided in 328 to lift the exile of Arius. What had been devised as a political tranquilizer complicated the situation even more now. Athanasius, having succeeded bishop Alexander in the same year, refused to home Arius in his diocese, a stance that now in turn infuriated the emperor. So Athanasius had to go into exile; for obvious reasons he chose Rome and continued to lambast Arianism with the active support of the church in the West which had no problems with the „homousion". Constantine died over this protracted battle; as a matter of irony it was an Arian bishop, his friend, who baptized him before his imminent death in 337. Almost at the same time Arius died, shortly before his reinstatement into his old office in Alexandria.

After the death of Constantine the situation became even more bizarre. Emperor Constantius declared a general amnesty; all convicted participants - of either side - were allowed to resume their old offices. Very soon it became apparent that Constantius preferred the Arians, however. Their side received the most influential bishoprics, securing them as the staunch supporters of the emperor. In addition the confines of the bishoprics were made identical with those of the administrative provinces.

The indefatigable firebrand Athanasius meanwhile had succeeded in the convocation of a synod at Rome in 340 which declared him and his supporter Marcellus of Ancyra to be within the decrees of Nicaea, i.e. orthodox. The East was not slow in responding. In the following year a synod at Antiochia anathemized Athanasius and Marcellus.

Constantius was governed by the same principle as his father: disunity in the church spells disaster for the empire. In order not to let the rift widen he called a synod at Sardes in 342, with a result to the contrary: in the face of the emperor both sides anathemized each other. Considering the known preference of the emperor towards the Arians the orthodox side saw its cause lost already.

Constantius however had to fight a war with Persia and needed unity at all theological cost. He urged the moderate Arians and the Origenistic majority to strike up a compromise with the Western church. They complied, Athanasius could return to his see in 346.

Seven years later the emperor had his back free again and saw no need any more to cajole the factions into compromises. He called a synod at Arles in 353 and at Milan at 355 which ended in the anathema to the „homousios". In 356 the cathedral of Athanasius in Alexandria was stormed by imperial soldiers and Athanasius had to flee - but where to? Rome was barred to him so he took to the desert.

Again the cause of the „Nicaeans" seemed lost. This time, however, they were saved by the opposition party. Unity in the Arian camp existed only as long as the inclusion of the iota was the target. Having finally reached this goal they split into three factions: the radical Arians, the basically anti-Arian Origenists and a compromise group under the imperial court bishops Valens and Ursacius.

The fight had long ago ceased to be the issue of Arius. The number of Non-Arians who were also objecting to the creed of Nicaea had considerably increased; the Origenists called for a greater part of reason against mysticism, into which they rated also the notion of a Trinity.

As the infighting went on Julian, called Apostate (The Defector), became emperor. We will meet him in one of the following chapters so we confine ourselves here to say that he wanted to see the church break finally apart over its fight. His two years of pagan reign however taught the Nicaeans that the adversaries were certainly not only the Arians. So instead of mutual dismembering they chose a course of reconciliation on the basis of common interests, and closed ranks.

In 362 there convened another synod in Alexandria - under whom but Athanasius? But his tempestous life in and out of exile may have had a mollifying effect on him: he accepted a personal difference between Father, Son and Holy Spirit. In addition to that he even consented to reduce the „homousios" to mean „same", instead of the former „identical". Now also the Origenists could accept the Nicaean formula. The radical Arians had been largely silenced by that.

There is a strong need now to end the story. The last try to set the Arian belief over others was made by the emperor Valens. The two factions that had made peace in Alexandria, however, stood their ground and convinced the emperor to retract on his impulse. In 380 the emperor Theodosius finally decreed the Nicaean creed to be the only valid formula of faith, which was ratified one year later by the synod of Constantinople.

Arianism, however, was not dead; it continued to live for more than 200 years after. The reason was that Wulfila, the bishop and missionary of the Goths, was Arian. The Goths remained Arian, therefore, disregarding the theological feuding over the issue in the Roman Empire. Only when they were allowed as members into the crumbling empire in 382, together with other Arian German tribes, their faith slowly changed in generations to the now unified orthodox side, until the end of the Goths and Vandals toward the end of the 6th century.

# THE DISCUSSION

W: Every time I read Arius´ideas and the turbulences they have provoked I end up completely dissatisfied, in several respects. For one, Arius played the hyperbolic game of theologians, there and after, who believe indeed that they can come near to the „nature" of the God that had spoken through Yeshua, by biological synonyms, time, cause and effect ...

B: Stop here, please. If we do not share the opinion of Aristotle that the Creator is, as he called it, the un-moved mover or the un-caused cause, you end up in the inquiry of something „behind" him. Not in a backwards arrow of time, of course, because our time began with the creation of this cosmos and anything before it is simply not debatable. So much for cause!

W: I agree that I was not precise enough. Of course we believe that the Creator is the final cause, imaginably so also the cause of many more universes than ours. When I mentioned the term cause/effect I was referring to Arius who saw it working not only along the arrow of time in the cosmos but also working, by human hyperbole, also „within" God, especially when out of this God the „Logos" appeared, before the creation of our universe.

B: Now I see your point. The birth defect in our thinking about this phenomenon is that we applied the human term „person" to it. In doing so we ended up in analyzing the „relations" between God and Logos. Since we believe that it was the Logos who spoke from Yeshua, who prayed and asked to a „Father" we see indeed subordination, as Arius did. The murky notion of an identical or similar „substance" to or with the „Father" is the second pitiful attribute which we amoebae thought up. Or can you tell me what is the substance or essence of God?

W: How should I, or any created being? But you were interrupting me when I was trying to tell you why I am so dissatisfied with Arius. The second point is that Arius never bothered to separate the Logos from the man Yeshua; he subscribed to the tradition that human and divine „nature" are inextricably interwoven in his personality. This inevitably led him to the fatal imprecision that the Christ is the Logos, the human Yeshua included.

B: He can be forgiven in that, I think. The idea of the Logos as the interpreter of God to the creation, and not acting sequentially from one intelligent habitat to the next, but as the ever-ready „idea" of the Creator to which any reflexive population can connect, and which communicates through a representative of their own - this of course was completely beyond the insight of Arius and all of his contemporaries ...

W: - and also most of our contemporaries, we have to add.

B: Apparently so, but we must not get side-tracked. Any more reason for being dissatisfied with Arius?

W: By heart he was a scholastic in the bad sense, i.e. loosing the grand view over unfathomable and yet unimportant aspects, unimportant in the sense that they block the view on the essentials of the revelation: God is, God cares, God gives, God wants something from us in exchange - that is, if our free will is interested in his message. Compared to this central view what do I care about things which are forever barred from human understanding such as a Logos, a possible duality, trinity, subordination or not - I simply rejoice in the almost incredible fact that I, the amoeba, shall have an existence in the Creator after my bodily death. Non confundar in aeternum - I shall not perish in eternity - ! Constantine was right in his letter to Alexander and Arius:
„... a portion only of a question, in itself entirely devoid of importance ... actions worthy of inexperienced children ..." and so on. I am fully of his opinion.

B: You almost got carried away in your TeDeum, but I share your sentiment. The revelation through Yeshua is not to be rated less in any because a not omniscient and therefore possibly subordinate Logos communicated it to us. For us he is a part of God, but just what part is of no importance.

W: You are very Origenistic in your arguments, did you notice that?

B: No, I am not. I am just knowing my place in the scenario, something that apparently Origen forgot as well as Arius and Athanasius, not to mention later „christian" thinkers, up to our times.

W: Coming back to the events around Arius, where is the catch?

B: The deplorable and despisable fact is that the young christian church was corrupted by the state. It never recovered from this sweet poison.

The revelation through Yeshua as a commanded state religion, rejection or deviation from it a capital crime hence, mixing secular power politics unabashedly with the faith, mutually guaranteeing or gambling the existence of throne and altar, fanaticism, intolerance and crime against humanity in its wake for centuries - these are the viruses of the fatal asphyxiation process which we are monitoring today and which started then.

W: You forgot evolution.

B: Indeed I did. Where is room for evolution if religious thinkers write volumes on subtle or incomprehensible aspects of the revelation instead of trying to apply the essence of it to the real world, to blast a breach in the wall of geopolitics through which respect, understanding, pity and love can enter? Evolution of reason that occurs in the brain only without an impact to realpolitik is no evolution. It is only a concept thereof.

W: I think that Constantine was a very good example of realpolitik, no?

B: And what did he change, tell me, or Constantius or Theodosius? The only thing that interested them was the inner cohesion of a multi-ethnical empire. The Caesarian cult that had held it together for a few centuries was crumbling, so a new religion that had proven its tenacity inspite of numerous persecutions was ushered in. But she, as the old cult, was only an end towards a mean.

What they could not foresee of course was that the christian church, within a short time, would have the emperors depending on her.

W: I think that both of us were evading so far the crucial question: Has Arius contributed to evolution or not? Have his views been vindicated in the light of our times, or not?

B: These were two questions, not one. I am trying to give my view in good Origen style now: Yes, he has contributed to evolution and if it is only by the fact of standing up against a powerful faith organization. This alone earns him evolutionary respect, no doubt.

What is more, he raised the flag of reason on the buttresses of scripture, insisting that increased human insight has to be rated higher than mysticism.

And now the „No": No, because he failed to recognize the fallibility of human insight. Another „no" for his undertaking to question into the nature, essence, being, or whatever you call it, of the Creator. He only came to conclusions what could n o t be the case, but his teachings lack any positive elements that could be utilized for building a better church, let alone a better mankind.

His scholastic fanaticism got the better of him. The iota meant more to him apparently than the peaceful coexistence within an otherwise congruent creed. He took one side and proclaimed it as the only truth. The chance that two possible truths can give satisfactory insight into one problem was ruled out by him.

W: So he was a great thinker, but in the end a great failure?

B: The distance between the two has always been of the width of a hair only.

# EMPEROR JULIAN

## 332 - 363

# THE MAN

(332 - 363)

Reaction - there are a lot of synonyms to this one word. In physics we know since Newton that no action is possible without reaction; in chemistry a reaction means something different altogether. In the general and neutral sense it refers to the response of a living being to something that is influencing or confronting it.

To be reactionary, however, has developed an altogether different meaning in the last centuries. It has become the label of disdain which - in their own opinion - progressive persons or movements are pinning on those persons or groups thereof which are not only conversative, i.e. adherence to the use of principles that have proven their value, but which are actively trying to bar progress, to roll back developments; not a loyal opposition that has a different solution to a shared problem, but somebody who is militantly fighting to regain lost ground, geographically or spiritually, and that with a blatant disregard for humanity.

A so-called christian history has tried to pin just that label on Emperor Julian, Flavius Claudius Iulianus with his full name, who was the nephew of emperor Constantine and was born in the year of 332 in Constantinople. This attempt for defamation of character should not astonish anybody who is interested in history because it is always the victor who writes it.

As the full name of Julian shows he came from the highest stratum of Roman nobility. When he was 3 years old emperor Constantine thought it was better to assign the empire to his heirs now instead of having civil war after his death because of a missing testament. The same folly should be repeated 500 years later by Charlemagne and with the same disastrous results.

Constantine´s sons, Constantine II, Constantius and Constans were assigned the bulk parts of the empire, the two nephews had to be content with Greece, Makedonia and Armenia, not exactly an opulent legacy compared to the sons´ share.

The volcano erupted immediately after Constantine's death in 337. Allegedly Constantius had persuaded the army generals not to recognize any other authority but those of the sons of the dead emperor, his in the first line. Consequently, all his other male relatives were murdered, which should have included Julian and his brother Gallus as well. Why Constantius spared the life of the two boys is not known; also Ammianus, the court historian, gives no clue. While Constantius fought another war with the arch-enemy Persia his two brothers went for each others throats in a protracted civil war which neither survived. In 353 Constantius found himself to be the sole emperor. But was he really unchallenged while his two nephews were alive?

The father, the eldest brother and most of the cousins of Julian were murdered in the civil war. In the midst of this turmoil Julian was sent to Eusebius, the bishop of Nicomedia, where he was introduced to christian theology and, by his tutor Mardonius, into the world of Homer. Apparently Julian liked Greek mythology then there already more than christian mysticism.

Why Constantius banned him at the age of 9 together with his brother Gallus to Kappadokia's castle of Macellum is not known. They spent six years there on which there is no mentioning from Julian himself later or from any third source.

When the ban was lifted, again for reasons unknown to us, Julian was allowed to reside in Constantinople. But the 15 year old youth apparently radiated all the natural charms of his age and education in the palace, more than the suspicious Constantius could digest. So he was again sent to the near Nicomedia, very probably his own selection of an exile resort, as long as he had the choice.

It was unavoidable that in his dangerous age of seventeen he should embrace philosophy. And as he immersed his pliable mind into the ideas of the great thinkers he, the baptized christian, was ever more irked by the noise, intolerance and brutality which the various christian factions hurled at each other on the pulpits and streets during the years of the hot Arian dispute.

His elder brother Gallus was appointed Cesar in 351 by Constantius, i.e. to be his follower-designate. No imperial honour was bestowed on Julian, however. Apparently the spies whom Constantius employed reported that the young man was not showing any political ambitions, which was the plain truth. Julian changed from Nicomedia to Pergamon and Ephesus; it was especially his teacher Maximus in Ephesus who helped him to rearrange his set of values in the direction of an enlightened paganism as the preferable substitute for a strife-torn Christianity.

Three years later his brother Gallus had managed to have the Asian provinces in an uproar by governing them with an unheard-of cruelty which the emperor apparently was too slow to notice. Gallus, and also Julian, were summoned to Milan in 354. Gallus was tried, convicted and beheaded, in order to affirm imperial justice to the restive Asian provinces.

Julian had been put under house arrest and stayed so for several months, awaiting a likely fate. Constantius must have had several conversations with him, otherwise he would not have come to the conclusion that Julian posed no danger to his rule. But still he thought it wiser to have the young man in a safe distance to the temptations of the court and in 355 consented, to Julian's ill concealed joy, to exile him to Athens.

These six months must have been the most endearing in his life to him. Walking in the academies that had heard Platon and Aristotle, making friends with the leading philosophers of his time - it was there that he most acutely felt the difference of quality between an educated paganism and the riotous rule of the priest-led christian mob, not to speak of the murderous ambiente prevailing around the throne.

Ammian reports that he came to the conclusion that no beasts were more ferocious than Christians. In this state of mind he yielded to the urging of his teachers to be initiated into the Mysteries at Eleusis, a pagan cult which of course revealed no mysteries but claimed to the way to attain, in many stages, the mystic spiritual union of the self with the Eternal Principle. It was a dangerous move for a baptized prince; had any of the savants spoken publicly on it, Julian's fate would have been sealed. But Julian and his friends were confident that time would work for them.

It worked almost too fast. Six months after his arrival in Athens emperor Constantius sent for him. Counting the facts Julian was sure that his Eleusinic adventure had been reported to the emperor so he prepared to hide instead. The empress Eusebia however sent him a message telling him that he had nothing to fear; she also knew nothing about his inner conversion to paganism when she spoke for him to the emperor. So Julian went to Milan again, in 355.

Eusebia must have spoken very well indeed. Constantius gave his sister Helena into marriage to Julian; marrying his own aunt certainly was not the at the top of Julian´s desires, but there was no choice than to accept the political matrimonium. To everyone´s surprise it turned out to be a model marriage until the death of Helena and Julian never ceased to mourn her; he did not marry again after.

Constantius´recall of Julian really had another target. He wanted to put Julian to a political acid test. Constantius gave him the title of Cesar and ordered him to secure the province of Gallia.

During the civil wars over Constantine´s heritage the Alemannic tribes on the Upper Rhine had correctly sensed their chance to tear into what is now Alsace-Lorraine, to sack Cologne after having defeated a Roman army and to capture dozens of other borderline towns. Why Constantius gave the task of saving and reorganizing Gallia to a relative who had neither military training nor organizational experience remains a mystery. One thing may be considered to be sure: he was not feeling that he sent Julian to certain doom, because the realpolitician in him was quite aware of the fact that a ruin of Julian´s expedition would spell the complete loss of the province, and, subsequently, an extraordinary cost to the empire to regain from the invaders again.

Although history does not name them, Julian apparently was assisted by experienced army troupiers and spent the time in winter quarters at Vienne (Rhone Valley) with steeling his body and learning the tactics of war. 356 saw Julian the general; he drew together an army at the town called Reims today, gave battle to the German invaders, beat them and recaptured Cologne.

The Alemanni encircled him at (today) Sens but he managed to feed and defend the city for thirty days, until they withdrew. Following them south he met their main army at (today) Strasbourg. Developing the phalanx attack formation of the Greek into a better cutting crescent wedge formation of infantry Julian led his outnumbered army to victory, not only due to superior tactics but by also exposing himself constantly to danger within the fighting, inspiring his soldiers as nobody had done before him.

From this day onward Julian was and remained the idol of his army as only Julius Caesar was before him. For good measure, Julian routed the Franks in the valley of the Meuse and forced them back over the Rhine. Now Gallia was freed in the military sense, but the tasks of putting agriculture back on its feet in the devastated parts of the country, restoring travel safety, fomenting artesanal production and trade in and among the cities and at the same time earning taxes for financing provincial and central government remained. Julian succeeded in five years of dedicated labour at this goal, fortifying also the defence lines along the Rhine - and reducing taxes inspite of all this.

His fame did not halt there. As the supreme judge in Gallia he also brought common sense and humanity into the lower courts. One incident is just too significant not to be told. We owe the story to Ammianus:

„Numerius, a former governor of Gallia Narbonensis, was charged with embezzlement. He denied the charge and could not be confuted at any point. The judge Delfidius, exasperated by the lack of proofs, cried out to the presiding Julian: „Can anyone, most mighty Cesar, ever be found guilty if it be enough to deny the charge?" To which Julian replied:" „Can anyone be proved innocent if it be enough to have accused him?" These pillars of justice, the defendant being deemed innocent until conviction and the burden of proof resting on the accuser, are upholding justice in all democratic countries of the world still today.

We are jumping imperial court cabale which, in the end, denied Julian a son. By ineptitude or bribery the midwife cut the navel string of the newborn too close to the body so that the child bled to death. So will have done the midwife.

Now again history was repeating itself. Constantius fought with the Persian king Shahpur over the Roman provinces Mesopotamia and Armenia. In order to amass an army that would balance the Persian force Constantius sent imperial delegates to the Western provinces with orders to the governors, to Julian also, to give them 300 soldiers from each regiment to be marched to the Persian front. Loyally to the end, Julian wanted to comply; the soldiers, however, who had enlisted on the understanding that they would not have to serve south of the Alps or Pyrenees, refused by surrounding Julian´s palace and acclaiming him Emperor. He admonished them to retract the title and themselves, which of course they did not, for a simple legionary can smell a true leader faster than hordes of politicians. Another Rubicon opened before Julian´s feet; with a heavy heart he waded into it.

Constantius heard of the coup d´etat when he was still engaged with the Persians in Kilikia. After fighting Shahpur for one more year he felt that he had to decide between winning the war or losing the empire. He struck up a truce with king Shahpur I and marched westward, for one more fratricidal combat between Roman legions.

This time fate came to the rescue of Julian. While he had put up camp near todays Belgrade, Constantius died in November 361; he had reached 45 years only. Julian entered Constantinople and assumed title and tasks of a Roman emperor by legal succession instead by civil war. At first, he was very welcome there.

When still on the march to meet Constantius Julian had written to his teacher Maximus: „We now publicly adore the gods and all the army that followes me is devoted to their worship." All christian insignia were removed from the legions´eagles.

Julian had suffered too much at the hands of a christian emperor or by the murderous camarilla of the Byzantine court that he could be fair now to christianism. His controlled anger was fomented, however, not by ideas of revenge for his murdered father and brother but much more so by the atrocities which the christian mobs and their leader priests and monks had inflicted on the life and property of innocent pagans. Most historians agree that in the roughly 100 years after Constantine´s decree of tolerance, but especially in the years of civil war after his death more pagans were slaughtered by fanatic christian mobs than christians by all imperial persecutions ever before.

As a matter of irony it was not only christians against heathens but also one christian sect against the other: Arians, Non-Arians, Nestorians, Pelagians, Donatists, Doketists and a long trail of other „ists" tore each other to pieces, verbally and literally so on the streets of the cities. What united them was the pilfering and destruction of pagan temples and the killing of their priests and faithful. Julian compared the christian lot to ferocious beasts but insulted all animals by that.

Julian´s immediate actions as an emperor were swift, therefore. He ordered that the destroyed temples had to be rebuilt at the cost of the christian churches. But he allowed the christian faith full freedom of preaching and worship and he reinstated the orthodox bishops who had been exiled by Constantius. On the spoils of the faith, however, he stepped down with an iron foot: the tax exemption for the clergy was lifted, testaments in favour of the church were made null and void. He barred christians from civil service and from teaching rhetorics or philosophy. He permitted the demolition of christian churches that had been built illegally over the ruins or on the land of pagan temples.

His actions had an unintended effect. For a while the christian factions forgot their infighting and united against Julian, whose cold strategy of course had again manifest injustice in its wake as is always the case when a ruling organization declares a flat anathema on all opposition. There were riots against Julian´s decrees, of course; to nobody´s surprise rioting christians were severely punished, rioting pagans were let off with clemency.

What is more, Julian wrote a theological pamphlet „Against the teachings of the Galilees" - the word used by him for christians. In his childhood Julian had to absorb an overdose of christian teaching and knew the Scriptures up and down. Since the church had discarded Markion´s demands to cut out the Hebrew part of the religion, Julian, as most other free-willed thinkers after him, tore into the so-called Old Testament, exposing the mysticism of the Genesis and the inconsistency of an almighty and omniscient God against the man-painted Yahveh. He was not kinder to the four reports on Yeshua, of which he esteemed only John´s rendition because he recognized many of Platon´s ideas in it.

Christian historians and, of course, theologians of all later times have tried to paste the label „reactionary" on Julian, „Apostata", the Defector from true faith and a „persecutor" of the christians. A defector he was, and gladly so in the face of a man-despising christian church. A persecutor of christians he never was, but a sworn enemy of their fanaticism and intransigence. He had become too much of a philosopher than to indulge in the wholesale persecution of other creeds, even of such a debased lot as the Galilees in his opinion.

He organized a pagan church with himself as the pontifex maximus, exhorting his priests to teach without rancor, to distribute alms to all needy people and to grant hospitability to travelers. There is a letter from him to his priests in the empire, which is a Magna Charta of priest-pontifex relationship plus a lot of intrinsic „christian" concepts on how to deal with the poor, helpless and even wicked.

As Durant is aptly remarking, this pagan was a Christian in everything but creed.

Julian´s ascetic life won him no friends. He disdained the theatre, found racing in the Hippodrome boring after a while and had cleaned out the imperial court upon his arrival of all the human trash that usually accumulates in a „Byzantine" atmosphere. His beloved wife Helena died of reasons unknown before he had returned from Gallia and it is said that he stayed sexually austere ever after; the accounts we have of his bodily needs would send shudders along the spine of most monks; it is very believable, also on his philosophical basis.

It is high time to close the life account on Julian here, inspite of so many missing dabs of color on the canvas. As before him Constantius also Julian considered the Persians to be a constant threat to the empire. He gathered his troops in Antiochia in 362 and led the army across the Euphrates and Tigris in 363. The army became ever more exhausted by the „scorched earth" policy of the Persians which left no grain, wells, cattle or roofs to the advancing enemy.

Extricating his army from a trap into which the Persians had led him with great psychological cunning, Julian, riding in pursuit without his armor, had a javelin pushed in his side, piercing his liver. He died in best Socratian style, discussing the immortality of the soul with his beloved philosophers Maximus and Priscus. It was on the 27th of June 363; he had lived for thirtyone years only.

It is remarkable that no Persian claimed the prize which Shahpur had put on the life of Julian, so rumors persisted that he had been slain by a christian hand, an opinion which also Libanius adopted. It never was proved, but still appears as a logical possibility.

The army chose Jovian, the captain of the imperial guard, to be the new emperor. He returned to Shahpur four of the five provinces which Diocletian had robbed two generations before and made a lasting peace. Jovian was christian, he restrained himself however; he withdrew state support from the pagan temples and lifted all of Julian´s decrees that had disadvantaged christian believers or their organization. There was no persecution of pagans, however, and there are no reports that celebrating christian mobs went on another rampage, constrained apparently by now reasonable Christian leaders.

# THE DISCUSSION

B: Thirtyone years. He endured for sixty and developed wisdom for ninety in his life. In hindsight it is a marvel that he did not break down, or when in power, did not unleash a campaign of terror against the Galilees whom he utterly despised. Nobody could have stopped him.

W: The christian historians, up to our days, claim that he did just that. Of course not Nero-style, more subtle and therefore more hurting to them all, creating second-class citizens who got the short end of justice in all courts. I have registered the sarcasm in his comments where e.g. the infighting of christian factions had produced turmoil in Edessa, whereupon Julian confiscated the assets of the church and distributed the proceeds among his soldiers:

> „It is me who is the true friend of the Galilees because their marvelous teaching promises the kingdom of heavens to the poor. By my help the christians have been alleviated from the burden of wordly goods. They now will pursue the parth of virtue with ever greater endeavour."

B: I cannot but put a „How true!" on his letter.

W: Caution, my friend. Julian´s action was clearly illegal.

B: No, it was not. Disputed property had been sequestered by the state. How the state, or Julian, spent the proceeds rests with his superior judgement. Finish.

W: But you can almost see the grin on his face when he wrote this letter, no?

B: Very much so, but let us call it a philosopher´s smile, then we agree. I know that you are not taking the orthodox side, because Julian the man, the philosopher, the believer in a Final Divine Being can only be seen soaring over his time, very well registering the reckless anti-humanitarian stance of the Galilean creed, seeing on the other hand the situation of the empire, which meant most to him.

W: Sorry to pull you down from your eagle´s view. Julian never had any intention to let the Galilees gain influence, be it spiritually, nor it politically. The idea of the polis, the ideal community, did not govern Julian´s mind for a second because he knew since boyhood what utterly ruthless and murderous elements constituted a Byzantine court. The „dream", if we can put it in these terms, was harshly cornered in by defending the frontiers of the empire and by the insight of all imperial rulers, whatever their time, creed, ambition: not to trust anybody but yourself. And so he went down in history: a consummate philosopher, one of the most able administrators of his time, and a hated heretic to all christianity ever onward.

B: Is Julian a heretic in our rating? He did not object to a tenet of faith but to the creed as a whole. A religion to which he was tied since he was able to think or speak. He discarded all that in his mind, and when he felt safe to speak, also in the public eye.

W: When I am recognizing an attitude of evolution, and only this we are discussing here, I am called upon here to say in the case of Julian: YES, and in very capital letters, he was the evolutionary beacon of his times.

B: Let´s have your explanation of it, please!

W: Julian was skeptic of the scriptures in christian faith but this is not the reason why he held the Galilees in contempt. What was embittering and infuriating him was the real-life performance of those who claimed to be the protagonists of the christian cause, be it the bishops or the christian imperial court.

The christian scum which ravaged the temples under the open or covert leadership of their priests and monks was just like any other mob in Roman history, striking wherever the looting was tolerated. No, it was not this which turned him against the Galilean creed.

Two things worked together to form his hard line. The first was the intolerance of the christian organization from top to bottom, the militant and provocative attitude it developed under

Constantine already, because it became a needed and wooed supporter of the empire. It was not yet a declared state religion, this hubris was reserved for Theodosius, but it knew that it was on the winning side and acted accordingly, i.e. disregarding even the most basic humanitarian rules against the losing side and heating or condoning fanaticism against the disbelievers.

B: Do you mean to say that Julian saw them acting against their belief and against humanity?

W: Their belief meant nothing to him, but the stoic pagan and the serene philosopher in him recognized the christian organization for what it was: an aggressive, intolerant, murderous creed. Of course he knew the teachings of Yeshua; they had been repeated too often to him when he was a child. He was among the first to notice that the christian church had made a travesty of these teachings and was out only for one thing: power, here and now, and death to any that stood in her way.

B: Where is the evolutionary progress, please?

W: By calling a criminal organization to it´s this name, regardless whether it is a church or a wordly regime that turns the tables on humanity. This is Julian´s evolutionary contribution no. 1 to posterity. But there is also his second contribution: do not only condemn these organizations, but fight them actively and don´t be too squeamish about the legal aspect in it because criminal systems always have made their tailor-made laws.

B: So Julian was answering terror with counter-terror?

W: He could have unleashed the military machine any time, but he did it only to quell riots and not to eradicate christians. His corps of officers knew of course that they were expected to come down hard on the christian side of these unrests. Of course he was biased and showed this openly. But his philosophy was based on justice and fairness, something which the fledgling christian church had already struck from its vocabulary.

B: So it is. Twentyfive years later the trap for humanity in the christian church snapped shut forever. State religion and state government needed each other, so a disbeliever in any of the two systems automatically became the enemy of the other. And so it stayed for the next 1.100 years - an incredible development in retrospect, because this means roughly 33 generations who had to live under the whip of both.

W: What are today´s christian churches saying to that?

B: All of them shrug it off as an inevitable historical development, certainly not free of errors - the word „crime" does not come over their lips -, the whole thing involved in the mysterious ways of God which we must not dare to fathom.

W: Have they shown any unconditional signs of repentance over their crimes along the centuries?

B: Not one of them, and of course not the mummified catholic church. Just recall the jesuitic wording of their apology to Galilee some ten years ago. It makes you want to vomit.

W: Coming back to Julian: did he have a chance to stop this development?

B: No, and he knew it. A gore-spilling persecution of the christians was not compatible with his moral belief and besides he was intelligent enough to see from such criminal actions before his time that this was certainly not a promising way to stamp out a faith.

W: We leave Julian here with great respect. Your final word for him?

B: He had the courage not to use power when he had it, a courage which all christian organizations missed: the opportunity for letting evolution enter.

# NESTORIUS

## ? - 460

# THE MAN

The heretics in the four preceding chapters may have been known already to the patient reader. But Nestorius? Who is he? Why is he included into this gallery of splendid - in the sense of the word - shining personalities? There is good reason indeed to do so. But before we are centering on Nestorius we must dig a little earlier and also relatively deeply, otherwise the stance of Nestorius will not develop its importance before our eyes.

The dispute was trod loose by Arius. The arcane crutches which the councils found for a nature of the „Logos" did not consider to the end what Yeshua´s nature was like. The methodical mistake which had crept into the discussion was that everybody reasoned about a „Christ", which means "The Anointed One" in Greek, referring to the sacred ointment that Hebrew kings received upon their coronation - but that was all.

It may be recalled that Paul very readily used this synonym also, which, in its essence, was always pointing to the mysterium of the Logos, certainly not to Yeshua the man. After the councils formed their questionable consensus on the „nature" of the Logos it was an inevitable step further to lay down the law on the „essence" of Yeshua. With that the famous - or rather infamous -"christological struggle" of the 4th century broke loose. The word „struggle" has been chosen deliberately because the term „dispute" would not nearly cover the intransigence nor „theological" ramifications that erupted over that issue.

The Arian explosion had showed that the Logos was part of the Creator, with or without the iota. But this Logos spoke from the human male Yeshua, who, in the repulsive thinking of the Hebrews had to be killed in order to reconcile a treacherous world to its Creator. Hopefully the reader agrees that this Stone Age notion is not worth any discussion here.

But still, this Hebrew mortgage was passed on by Paul, very much so, but also by Peter who should have known better, and, of all persons, also by John who tried to reconcile the happenings to venerable gnostic concepts.

So, who is this Yeshua? went the question in the age of Nestorius. Three requirements had to be met:

First:     this Yeshua must be a „full" human being, because „half a man", i.e. human physique plus divine soul would mean only „half redemption". In this we notice that the „redemption" to be worked was the pivotal issue, something that the evolution of consciousness has laid to rest already with not so pious blessings.

Second:  This „Christ" has to be an integral part of God also. Because if not, one is back to the Arian dispute.

Thirdly:  The divine and human nature of the „Christ" - i.e. of Yeshua in his terrestrial being - have to be an entity, ex ovo, meaning that the fertilized egg in Miriam was already of this double nature. With that, Mirijam was not only the mother of Yeshua the human male but at the same time the „Mother of God".

To this, Nestorius objected categorically and went down in history as one of the most likeable heretics we can imagine.

The time of the reader is well invested to follow the historical developments.

Nestorius made it acid-clear: Mirijam, with all due respect, is only the terrestrial womb of Yeshua the man - and nothing beyond it. With this notion he immediately ran into the artillery of the „Marianists": Mirijam had been selected to be the genitrix of the human Yeshua in which the Logos had gone into already, well before the physical birth of him - ex ovo.

Cyril of Alexandria, he died around 444, was apparently quite in the tradition of the radical holders of his see and declared: „... there is only the humanification of God to see. He was manifested in Yeshua, so Mirijam is quite logically the genitrix of God."

It was not quite as simple, as not only one, but two councils had to show. In the first Cyril was condemned under the aegis of Nestor.

To nobody´s surprise the next council was carried by the lobby of Cyril of Alexandria and condemned Nestor.

Both councils were held in Ephesus in 431. Both parties, of course, turned to the emperor for his casting vote. The emperor may be praised by posterity: both opionions were correct, he said, but, for keeping the peace in the imperium, both protagonists are to loose their seats. For reasons unknown, Cyril later regained the favour of the emperor and was re-instated.

The final verdict came in 433. The Antiochian school won by saying that Mirijam is indeed the Mother of God. Nestor was delared „anathema" - heretic.

The few historical facts on Nestorius and his followers are not so discouraging, however: the followers of Nestorius bowed out of the imperial orthodox church in 433 and after the questionable council of Chalcedon in 451. They founded their own Nestorian-Syrian church, which still exists today, to the satisfaction not only of their own faithful but to the homage of all „Logos-struck" denominations that have sprouted on the „christian" phylum of evolution.

This story could have been carried on almost interminably as every reader of christian or rather cultural history would confirm; but it was not, because it should serve among all possible controversial tenets of orthodox christian faith only towards a better understanding of Mirijam, who is running the danger to be pushed into divinity, because of a Polish pope who was reared in the Mariolatry of his nation. He is trying this, now, here, in 1998, in dead earnest.

The unsettling fact is that he is prompted on in this by numerous national and international Marianic movements. So this church might have a Quadruplity to explain in future, where Trinity could not be expressed. The future, however, is graciously short for this. Thank God, very literally.

# THE DISCUSSION

W: I feel we were a little bit too short on Nestorius, because before and after him raged the discussion in the young church on the „christological" issue, of which he have only scratched the surface at best. And then the councils, each one a more beautiful beast of arrogance, imperial maneuvering, rivalry contests between the patriarchates, beautiful empresses if the name Pulcheria was not a joke, who were willing partisans of factions, the tensions between the West and East church - I think it is a fascinating gobelin of which I do not get tired to look at. *

B: I agree. The dubious fame of a leading theologian in these times could not be earned in any other way than to have been excommunicated once - but re-communicated, of course, in due time. But I do not think that our short book is the wall on which we could unfold this tapestry. If the reader should be interested to have more detail information on these turbulent years, he best turns to historians who were able to write synthetic, integral history, as e.g. our beloved Durant. If they turn to their theologians it´s their choice and fault, because in this boiling cauldron of time between the 3rd and 5th century any faction can find the arguments it needs, also for today´s discussions.

W: And what is our prime argument?

B: Delusion of grandeur was the basic mistake of this time - and still of our´s also. Inspite of accepting the essentials of the revelation through Yeshua everybody went wild on an ante mortem and post mortem of this man, his „nature", and how this fitted in with the stone-age idea of a necessary redemption of man from sin - having acted against the deity in a litteral or mystic sense - in short, the hunt was on as to which terrestrial passport should be issued to Yeshua: God, Man, or Mixture. The hubris went so far as to say that if Yeshua did not fit any of these permutations he could not have managed this so-called salvation.

W: This is quite interesting, but it detracts us from what we think, and we certainly do not invent a Sexuality. Even a Trinity is too much for us, anyway. What I wanted to say is that I am apalled to see hordes of old men at work, who did not have to pay for their meals any more, otherwise they would have been much more down to earth, but who dared to construct a grid system of their own which was to be the governing factor in the acceptance of the revelation through Yeshua - and not the other way round. The tail began to wag the dog - this language may be forgiven. The incredible arrogance that arose in these decades, decreeing that the revelation has to conform to the intricate and yet hopelessly terrestrial concepts of a human brain - otherwise it cannot be a revelation - this is in my opinion the leitmotif of all the future abominable theology that had its poisonous roots in just these times.

B: Well roared, lion! But we must get onward with our immediate hero, Nestorius. Was he „ungallant" to Mary, as Will Durant called it tongue - in-cheek, or was he more adamant?

W: Nestorius was crystal clear and we have to thank him for that. Mary is the mother of Yeshua. He did not say so, but his dictum included: And Yussuf is the father of Yeshua.

B: And we add: Yes, and more was not necessary.

W: So we are Nestorians?

B: My dear friend, if we wanted to link all the anathemized opinions of the so-called christian history we would end up with much more names of ours than the most „high" named princes of baroque times, at least 17 or so beforde our real names - a litany of shame to the orthodox mummies, a list of honour to us. But we are not arranging them here. In order to answer your question, however: yes, we are also Nestorians.

W: The deplorable difficulties which Mariolatry has brought into the centuries up to Luther - these we have mentioned in our first book and they need not be repeated here. But this incredible Polish Pope - is he really thinking to accord divine status to the obedient wife, mother, Mary?

B:   There are only two possibilities, here, towards the end of 1998:

No. 1: He dies before trying, and with no regrets from us.

No. 2: He dares to elevate Mary to deity status, against all human reason. This only will hasten the demise of the so-called priest churches of „christian" denominations, be they subscribers to his dogma or not.

W:  Hearing you we could only wish that this Polish Pope would come forward to decree Mary a Godess?

B:   I hope not. In fact, and God may forgive me, I hope that he dies before he issues this monstrosity. But, if he should do so, the terminal fight is on which only accelerates the death of the so-called „christian" priest-churches. So, flippantly speaking, he is welcome!

# JOHN WICLIF

## ~ 1320 - 1384

# THE MAN

The life of John Wiclif is an open book to posterity. The high profile which he immediately gained with his postulates and the exact reports on them were due to the fact that a good part of them carried also a politically explosive quality, not only in matters of faith or church organization. The question which had simmered for almost a hundred years now was asked increasingly louder in Wiclif´s time: to whom do we owe our prime allegiance, to the Pope or to our country?

Theological discussions prospered on this hotbed especially well. Attacks on dogmas and the organization had a thunder of their own, of course, but in combination with the increasing anti-papal feelings they also carried their good share of power politics as well, be it the discussion of the confessional, of purgatory and very much so the sale of indulgences, the postulate for a poor church and, consequently, a poor clergy - all of which was demanded by John Wiclif.

It is with good reason that historians see the heretical trinity of Wiclif, Hus and Luther as one unbroken line that is spanning two centuries. As bystanders we are asking ourselves why England had to wait for Henry VIII. to cut the tablecloth between the papacy and secular rule? Wiclif had produced the tools more than 100 years earlier.

He was born around 1320 in Hipswell, near to the village of Wiclif, Nothern Yorkshire. He studied and thereafter taught theology in Oxford. In 1360 we see him already in his prestigious post as head of the venerable Balliol College there. Being an ordained priest by that time he had also been assigned a city parish besides his academic duties.

We are turning to the political scenario first. Back in 1213 King John had consented to pay an annual tribute to the papacy on the grounds that England was claimed to be a papal fiefdom that was given as a lien only to the English kings.

King Edward III. and the nobility would have tolerated this questionable taxation for some time more were it not for the fact that the Pope had transferred his court to Avignon upon the „invitation" of the French king - with whom England was at war. But not only this money went to the enemy. Many French-born cardinals of the curia had a claim to the fat tithings of parishes and bishoprics in England; also these sums were shipped to France every year.

The English church on the other side strongly resisted any further taxation by the state beyond the tithing of its income. As long as the Upper House was ruled by a majority of prelates there was no legal way for the Treasury to change the situation.

Small wonder, therefore, that the anti-clerical resentment grew among the secular nobility on the King´s Court. In 1333 Edward III. declared the tribute arrangement between King John and the curia to be null and void. The year of 1351 saw the Statute of Provisors which did away with the appointment of clerics and apportioning of tithes by the Pope. This was followed by the first Statute of Praemunire which forbade seeking redress before papal courts if the issue was, according to the King, subordinate to secular justice.

The unabashed leader of the anti-clerical party at the Court was the son of Edward II., John, Duke of Lancaster, who was called John of Gaunt because of Gent, his city of birth. If it had not been for his constant protection of Wiclif then the brave priest would have gone down in history as a martyr well before John Hus.

When Parliament renewed its resolution in 1366 not to pay the infamous tribute to the curia any more it asked Wiclif to draw up the writ of justification for this move. He was also nominated to be part of the royal delegation which negotiated on the abolition of the tribute with the curia in Brugge, July 1376. In September of the same year he gave the theological blessings and legal rationale to the intentions of John of Gaunt to sequester a sizeable part of the church property.

From these years onwards Wiclif was the bête noir of the clerical party, more hated than John of Gaunt. To the bishop of London,

Courtenay, it was evident that he could not penetrate the protective cover by any wordly means which the Duke had granted the rebel priest. So he resorted to the only weapon he could wield over Wiclif: the accusation of heresy.

In February 1377 Wiclif was ordered to appear before a Church Council in St. Paul´s church. He appeared, but with him John of Gaunt, accompanied by his armed guards. Before any theological arguments could be exchanged the guards had broken loose a heated fist fight with the delegates. In the ensuing meleé the bishop had no choice but to cancel the meeting.

But Courtenay was a tenacious man, and clever. He presented to Pope Gregor XI. an anthology of 52 allegedly heretical texts taken from the prolific writings of Wiclif. The Pope confirmed 18 of them to be truly heretical and ordered the English bishops to have Wiclif arrested and chained until further orders. Fearing the temper of John of Gaunt, however, even bishop Courtenay decided not to try anything so rash.

The situation became ever more strained by an expertise which the new Parliament and the royal advisers asked from Wiclif on the „legitimacy of withholding the wealth of the kingdom so as not to transfer it abroad even if the Pope ... should demand that upon imposition of penalty?" The English treasury was as good as empty, the French king prepared for an invasion of England - what foolishness to have papal collectors in England who delivered the money to a French Pope and a curia in which there was a French majority?
The wording of the task that was entrusted to Wiclif´s pen was clearly a leading question which Wiclif would not have needed to come up with the correct legal answer.

Wiclifs expertise was devastating, tantamount to a declaration of war by England against the curia. Looking back and knowing everything better afterwards we may be allowed to say that then and there was the time to cut the relations between the papacy and the State of England for good, over causes much more honourable than over hapless queens that had fallen out of royal grace and were executed.

Wiclif, of course, wanted exactly this to happen. He recommended an independent State Church. This statement, however, was so revolutionary that even the supporters of Wiclif, inclusively John of Gaunt, forbade him any more elaborations on this issue. England had to wait indeed for Henry VIII.

But also the purged text of Wiclif´s expertise was too much for the papacy now. It turned its ultimate weapon against him: excommunication and ban. On December 18th 1377 the orthodox English bishops published the papal bulla of anathema on Wiclif. With that they also requested the Chancellor of the Oxford University to jail Wiclif. Oxford presented a shining example 700 years ahead to Tuebingen by sidestepping the papal damnation of one teacher.

The University of Oxford had abolished the rights of the episcopate to meddle in university matters. So the majority of the professors either openly supported Wiclif´s views or held up at least his right to proclaim them with impunity. At the same time, being familiar with the covert ways of the curia, they advised Wiclif to adopt a low profile for a while.

The other side, however, kept pressing their issue. In March 1378 Wiclif was called to appear before the synod of English bishops at Lambeth, to which he obeyed. The protagonist bishops Courtenay and Sudbury had realized too late, however, the mood in the royal court and that of the street. A clandestine letter of the Queen-Mother had warned them already not to condemn Wiclif.

On the first day of the session a „mob" intruded protesting against inquisition methods in England. We are probably not too far off in surmising that the „mob" had been carefully orchestrated by John of Gaunt, Wiclif´s guardian angel. Wiclif returned free and triumphantly to Oxford.

Pope Gregor XI. died in the same year. His death entailed one of the greatest church schisms ever. In the lee of the uproar nobody cared for the revolutionary ideas of John Wiclif for some years. He used this spell to castigate the misuse and travesty of the revelation through Christ by an opulent and debased clerical organization.

With that we are coming to the second major area of his works which finally drew, inevitably so, the second broadside from the orthodox church.

The church organization, not so much at the level of the higher clergy but in the rank-and-file organization of priests and monks had deteriorated to a permanent fiesta of carnal amusement that had become the butt of English humor and scorn.

John Wiclif tore into them frontally. He accused the monks of preaching individual christian poverty but to amass collective riches for their monasteries. He raged against the sale of indulgences two hundred years before Luther. He demanded that illegal acts by the clergy should be tried before ordinary courts, especially so their seduction of maiden, women, widows. He exposed the parish priests „...to cozy up to the rich, to despise the poor, to readily forgive the trespasses of the well-to-do but to excommunicate the poor because of their delays in paying their tithes, to indulge in the joys of hunting and card games and to preach miracles that never happened ...“

Never before Luther was such a mirror held to the face of a corrupt clergy. His language was not less Lutherian. The comparisons drawn from a broad range of the fauna is in our opinion an insult to the animals. At his time, however, this was used to depict ultimate depravity.

John Wiclif´s recipé was very simple: the origin of all this filth is the amassing of secular wealth by priests, abbeys, bishoprics - the papacy goes without saying. Only a church that has divested itself of its wealth, with priests that have to work or to beg for their daily support - only this leads back to the teachings of Christ.

The cantus firmus of his convictions was that the secular government is sovereign in all wordly issues and not subject to papal authority as rammed through by Gregor VII. Hildebrand, the sinister German fanatic, or by Boniface VIII. Secular government is furthermore entitled to control church property and to instal the priests, he maintained.

Parallel to castigating the travesty of the faith organization he also zeroed in on a number of „unthinkable issues“. The confessional, Wiclif maintains, is only an instrument of power for the priests and has no biblical justification whatsoever. The „trans-substantiation“

of bread and wine is a human hyperbole. What is happening at these occasions is the „con-substantiality", i.e. Christ is present, but not in precisely the atoms of baked flour or pressed grape. Luther picked up from here.

John Wiclif, however, was a firm believer in pre-destination. Each human being is pre-ordained to his eternal fate, he might do for or against it what he wants - to no avail, not by faith, not by good works, he/she is „programmed" since eternity. It is deplorable for us that this brilliant spirit should subscribe to this utterly sordid concept which Paul created and Augustine perfected.

In June 1381 fate caught up with John Wiclif again. One of his earlier treatises was the famous „Tractatus de civili dominio - Treatise On Civil Propery". Man can own terrestrial property only in his capacity as an obedient follower of God. When in sin, however, i.e. in rebellion against God, this invisible property title expires. It may be taken from him and be given to those who are obedient to God.

But Wiclif, ever the radical, went further. Every just man or woman, he said, is only a trustee of God´s material things. It is imperative, he said 500 years before Karl Marx, that the God-fearing share all their property. This would eliminate a major source of evil, that of the striving to earn ever more capital - and that means power - by the individual.

In view of this teaching it is a matter of surprise that Wiclif had not been canonized in the socialist world, comparable to the also deserving Spartacus. Not one street bore his name in the socialist capitals. It probably was his connection of property and Divine Order which made it not acceptable as an instrument in the socialist creed.

Wiclif´s doctrine was viewed by the possessing part of the English population with a highly critical eye. It is reported that his life insurer John of Gaunt remonstrated sharply with him upon these anarchic demands.

June 1381 saw the uprising of a social revolution in England, sure enough. Every possessing faction, secular or clergy, wanted to save their nest eggs. So the flaming rhetoric of Wiclif, considered to be very christian before, was now considered to pave the way for sequestering legitimate property. The ranks against him closed instantly.

King Richard II. who almost lost his throne over the economic rebellion withdrew his protection from Wiclif. But the orthodox wolves who smelled their day were again thwarted by the staunch John of Gaunt who told Wiclif, 300 years before Galilee, to survive by shutting up. Upon his insistence Wiclif said a reluctant good-bye to martyrdom and settled in his parish of Lutterworth. The tithings thereof had been awarded to him decades earlier as a royal gratitude for his treatise on the relations of the State against the papacy.

But, straight out of a drama from Aischylos, things took a new twist. Bishop Courtenay was now the primas of the English Church, had condemned 24 theses of Wiclif in May 1382. With John of Gaunt still alive however he could not succeed farther than claiming, and getting, the revocation of Wiclif´s right to lecture at the Oxford University. Courtenay had wanted to see Wiclif burn but was denied the pleasure.

John Wiclif settled for good in Lutterworth, but not as a broken man. He kept turning out pamphlets against the depraved church as much as ever. In addition he instigated the formation of the „simple preachers", the Lollards, as they were known shortly. He instructed them to keep to the Scripture alone and not to possess anything. The scripture, he told them, rates more than any church dogma. In order to assist them in spreading their message he translated the bible into English, the New Testament by himself, the Old Testament followed 10 years later, done by his faithful Herdfore and Purvey.

Neither Avignon nor Rome had ever left Wiclif out of the curia´s sights. In 1384 Pope Urban VI. ordered Wiclif to Rome. The intent clearly was to start another court of inquisition on his allegedly heretic publications. God was more merciful. He lifted the personality of John Wiclif from his human encasing on December 31st 1384.

Preempting the story on his spiritual heir John Hus we are adding here that the Council of Constance, on May 4th 1415, ordered to tear John Wiclif´s remains from his grave at Lutterworth, to be thrown into the near river, and to burn all his papers, putting anathema on all his teachings, declaring him an all-out heretic.

John Wiclif must have looked down on them on this day with a forgiving smile that he hardly ever employed during his bodily life.

# THE DISCUSSION

W: When we are reading John Wiclif´s life it is as if we had three persons in one. There is the homo politicus and special adviser to the king, for whose fight with the Avignon curia and the French king he is producing convincing expertise. And then there is the flaming inside fighter against the corrupt church organization of his time. And finally there is the believer who dares to put reason to work against practically half of all sacrosanct notions on how God deals with man and how man should answer to God.

B: I agree that he has been one of the most lucid and outspoken minds of his time. All his struggle came from a basic feeling for humanity and fairness; the issues, however, were not of his invention. They were wide open for criticism, doubt or ridicule already when he was born; but he was able to address them in a superb and yet differing manner: cool logic and impeccable legal style in the writs for his king, uncontrolled rage when he was tearing into the debased priests, monks and monasteries, and with unassailable arguments in matters of faith, because he dared everybody to contest his opinions on the basis of the scripture.

W: You forgot the fourth element: the constant protection by John of Gaunt. Had it not been for this Duke then Wiclif never would have dared to become so outspoken also in matters of faith, because he knocked over more than half a dozen of sacred cows.

B: And there is a fifth element, the fearless attitude of the university of Oxford, its chancellor and professors when the high clergy tried to silence him.

W: Very much so. Now, what was the evolutionary contribution of John Wiclif in our opinion? Which one of the three is „our" protagonist?

B: By elimination I would say that his role of a political and theological adviser to his king carried little evolutionary impact. He was chosen because he was the best expert available among also doubtlessly highly qualified men on the Court.

W: Very much against any spiritual evolution is his adhering to the most un-godly and inhuman notion of predestination. It is absolutely inconceivable for the two of us that a mind that soared brilliantly over other important questions of faith should capitulate before this monstrosity?

B: I have no explanation for that either. It cannot be that he never was tempted because we read in so many places of his ideal of a humble and yet proud believer in God, needing no middlemen. But a proud believer is only the one who accepts the essence of the revelation in his free will, who is not trading in his conviction for blind hope. In all other respects John Wiclif was this proud-plus-humble believer, but not versus predestination. Very strange indeed.

W: I do not think that he swallowed his contrary opinion somewhere along his way. He was a reformer all through and could hardly be shushed up by John of Gaunt in the explosive issue of civil property. No, he earnestly believed in predestination, sorry.

B: Could it not be that he foresaw a complete breakdown of christianity also in its more noble parts if he assailed Paul and Augustine in this question?

W: Luther had no such inhibitions. We simply have to deal with the facts and one of these is that Wiclif saw no need to attack predestination. Finis.

B: Let us go on then in our search for the evolutionary element. He went squarely against the trade with indulgences, is this not evolutionary enough?

W: It certainly is a contribution to it if respected persons of their age come out openly against a corrupt faith organization, especially when they are still part of it and have to face trouble and danger therefore. In the same basket go Wiclif´s attacks on the depraved parish clergy and monks. In this he was the articulate spokesman of the majority of his contemporaries.

But I am saying with all due respect that this fight in itself is not enough to heave the human mind to a higher plateau from which he could draw a new vista of God And The World. Moreover we know that the so-called christian church, be it Catholic, Anglican, Lutheran or the orthodox organizations of the East were able to keep and transport their wealth over all periods of tribulation - up to our days. For them the Wiclif´s of their times were the barking dogs while the caravan plodded on.

B: Our procedure has eliminated the evolutionary impact of John Wiclif totally, apparently?

W: Not so, my friend. Not only has he contributed to an evolution in matters of faith, be it his discarding of a purgatory, of a confessional, of the priests middlemen role. Even his adherence to predestination cannot cloud this contribution. But his truly evolutionary achievement in my opinion was the foundation which he laid for a social revolution, not in isolated nations, but world-encompassing.

B: Practically the whole 20th century has seen the rise, decline and fall of the socialist empire. And you want to say that social revolution has not happened yet, world-wide?

W: This is exactly what I am saying, yes. And you were very correctly using the word „empire", because it was that and unabashedly so. But it was just another empire through which a new ruling class entered which was just as deftly exploiting the population as any feudal system before it - only the labels were changed. We have gone into this during our first book already, so we need not repeat the full argumentation here again.

B: Granted, but where is John Wiclif coming into this historical event?

W: Trouble is, he never came into it, because his ideas were too radical on one side and too christian on the other. Marx was denouncing the exploitation of man by man. Wiclif cut deeper. The first declaration of private property, the first fence built around a plot - they are the true reason of human misery. It is astonishing that it was not him who coined the phrase „property is theft".

He had it all laid down early in his life in his „Tractatus de civili dominio - Treatise on Civil Property". He said that every God-fearing person is the co-owner of all things with God. The just ones, therefore, have to possess and administrate all things jointly. But he did not stop here. There came a heavy dose of anarchism when he continued that personal property is against the order of universal virtues (against which Adam had sinned) and this order does not know of any man-made laws. He knew very well that he was on a collision course with Paul here. So in order not to preach outright revolution he pointed to a fake exit by saying that he was talking about a theoretical and ideal state of goods and minds.

B: Stop here for a moment, please. So Wiclif prepared convenient weapons for those who wanted to divest the church of its wealth, something which did not succeed, however, not in England nor anywhere else. John of Gaunt saw very acutely that also a theological incendiary can be used by social revolutionaries to set the world on fire. Wiclif very nearly succeeded when in 1382 the social revolution ripped England apart. Just as later on the German peasant rebellion pointed to Luther as its mentor so it was Wiclif here who was used as the ideological battering ram. He may have regretted ever to have written his treatise on civil property. You can still see the effects in the short and bizarre regime of the anabaptist movement in the German town of Münster. So I ask: evolutionary? No, thank you.

W: Wiclif knew that human nature was in the way, for him the inborn human inclination for sin. So in order to reach the desired status sin must be conquered first, which leads to the level of „just" personalities. A joint and just administration of the goods of this world would follow automatically. A world government of the world´s resources. I think it is a very evolutionary view indeed.

B: Not in my opinion, sorry. Gazing up to his ideal world he stumbled over very wordly rocks in his way. These were then, as in 1789 and today the notions of liberté, égalité and fraternité. Every adult today knows that these concepts cannot be had in one and the same system because they are mutually excluding each other.

If you raise liberty to the governing factor you lose the égalité, because since our species exists there have always been the more clever, more audacious, more industrious and, yes, also more unscrupulous who always have exploited their fellow humans. If you put equality forward, that is, enforce it, as John Wiclif had it in mind, you loose liberty and free will. And, I must confess, the brotherhood within a strictly egalitarian community must be utterly dull -

W: - if there is no love among them, yes. Only in this case you are right. If love were elevated to first place, or made the other side of the equation, then the three apparently incompatible terms would be a solution indeed.

We know today that the older formations of our brain are storing stone-age behaviour which breaks through in us seventy times per day. We shall not get rid of it in milleniums but if we let caring and love enter, over and above the triple slogan, then the concept of a common wealth and its common administration has - for the first time - a solid foundation and is not utopia any more. I confess that my knowledge of Wiclif´s treatise is limited and second-hand. Did he envisage this scenario?

B: Frankly, I also do not know. Apparently we destroyed the last such paradises more than 200 years ago in Polynesia. I grant you the proof, therefore, that these communities could very well exist.

W: Also in the absence of a church, apparently?

B: No. <u>Because</u> of the absence of a church, my friend! Before our posteriors shall have the luck to see such organism again - if ever - the so-called christian churches will have to die, and a few other non-christian priest organizations as well. Their agony has set in long ago, we are witnessing a passing part of the process but certainly not the end of it. But we believe in the evolution of human consciousness.

Who knows, two or three milleniums ahead there could wait a Wiclifian order of things after a phase of a highly beneficial chaos? It does not seem very probable as of today but who predicted relativity? Evolution cannot be pushed but pushes. With that I propose that we bow before John Wiclif. If we had only a handful of men with his courage here and now, in every major creed of this world!

# JOHN HUS

## 1369 - 1415

# THE MAN

After Richard II. of England had married Anne of Bohemia in 1382 the university of Oxford saw many students from Bohemia. Wiclif had died in 1384 but was very much alive in the institution which had long shielded him from the onslaughts of the papacy and the orthodox prelates of England.

When the students returned to Bohemia, to Prague mostly, they brought with them the scripts of Wiclif where they were eagerly copied and distributed. The soil for this seed was already prepared by national reform preachers like Konrad Waldhauser and John Milic who inflamed Prague with their accusations of the depravity of laymen and clergy alike.

Thomas Stitny who preached in Czech language was especially popular with his listeners because the use of the vernacular was implicitly always a rebuff towards the domineering and hated Germans. King Charles IV. had founded the first German university in Prague in 1347; under his reign the influx of French, Italian and German artists, scientists and above all administrators swelled to proportions which embittered the Czech nobility and burghers alike. The arrogant behaviour and opulent sinecures of the imports very soon became the object of hate by the Czech; the motifs underlying the later Hussitic wars were, therefore, a mixture of faith issues and a revolt against the foreign oppressive hierarchy.

In a jump over centuries this explosive ambiente was to become not only one of the preludes to the Thirty Years War; the oppressive Habsburg reign in the 19th century only fanned the hate. Hitler´s annexion of the young Czech state in 1938 was the last insult the Czechs wanted to take from the Germans.

The murder rampage and expulsion of approximately 1,5 million ethnical Germans in 1946 may be seen as the ultimate backlash of a development therefore whose seeds reached back prior to the time of John Hus. He, for them, was sent to the stake by a „German" council, because it convened in Constance.

Not one of the post-communist Czech Governments from 1989 onward could be moved by world opinion to indicate the slightest regret over the genocide of 1946 - for the Czech it was a balancing of accounts that was over-due for centuries. All this is told only to cast some light on the Czech psyche without any condoning of mass murder, expropriation or mass expulsion.

Back to the times of Hus: the emperor and the archbishop of Prague, the German Ernst, were sympathetic to the reformers and even gave them church and pulpit of their own, the Bethlehem chapel in Prague.

John Hus came from Husinec in Southern Bohemia and was a poor student of theology. In 1396 he was promoted to Magister and the year of 1401 saw him already as the Dean of the humanistic faculty at his alma mater. In the same year he was ordained to the priesthood, said a final goodbye to the merry student years and adopted a rigid ascetic life. Also he preached in the vernacular and became highly popular with the nobility and even Queen Sophia.

His monk-style life and his open support of Wiclif´s doctrine would have been enough already to infuriate the orthodox clergy. Since Hus continued however to openly attack their sybaritic ways of life the front against him grew ominous. The Bohemian prelates chose as their point of attack his adherence to the controversial theories of Wiclif, which were not yet condemned officially, but kept in a limbo of unspoken anathema by the orthodox, and, of course, by the Popes.

The exchange of arguments soon escalated to open warfare and the torrent of events swept Hus with them. From all accounts we have on him it cannot be said that he was of the same highly aggressive brand as his mentor Wiclif, but his enemies left him hardly a choice. So Hus who started out as a moral reformer very soon became the critic of ecclesiastic hierarchy, with the papacy in the first line and a decisive fighter against the abuse of faith that was degraded to the hand-maiden of secular church power: sale of indulgencies, rich monasteries and obscene monk life, the idolatry in the veneration of saints - practically the whole list of Wiclif´s themes.

In 1403 the Dome Chapter at Prague, being the administrative authority of the university, made an inquiry among the professors on the orthodox character of some 45 theses by Wiclif. A minority including Hus confirmed them. The majority, however, was of contrary opinion whereupon the professors were forbidden to discuss them publicly or privately. Most of them obeyed, but not Hus, as could be expected. Probably this muzzling of the university, which was in flagrant contrast to the brave resistance of Oxford, prompted Hus to double his efforts.

In 1408 the orthodox clergy of Prague demanded his silencing by archbishop Zbynek. The bishop who was sympathetic to Hus in the beginning asked him repeatedly to moderate his opinions, but Czech obstinacy plus holy furor could not brake Hus. And, above all, Hus had no John of Gaunt at his side. So Hus and some of his followers were excommunicated in 1409. Still not buckling in, however, they continued to preach and hold masses. This left the now irate archbishop with little choice, because now his power and credulity were at stake; he produced the ultimate weapon of the church: the interdict. No more masses, communion, sacraments, baptizing, weddings, burials, confessionals for the city of Prague. Moreover, the scripts of Wiclif in all of Bohemia were confiscated and burnt. Hus turned to the newly elected pope John XXIII. for redress, but received only a summons to the papal tribunal. On this shaky ground Hus decided not to travel to Rome.

The events culminated when the same pope started a new sales campaign for indulgences in 1411 in order to finance his „crusade" against the then King of Naples, Ladislaus. Now Hus and his closest ally, Hieronymus of Prague, pulled out all stops. Not only did they disregard the withdrawal of their right to preach but added a new calibre to their verbal artillery: the sales receipts of the trade with indulgences serve to finance the feudal murder of christians; the pope is the anti-christ. For good measure they denied the existence of a purgatory in order to let the absurdity of an indulgence shine brighter.

Most of the Bohemians sided with Hus in such aggressive manner against the papal salesmen that the King had to step in to protect their life. As could not be expected otherwise pope John XXIII. banned Hus & Co and threatened each city which would house them with the interdict. Apparently the King could convince Hus that the royal rule was endangered if this situation would last, so Hus, probably in order not to be guilty to have fostered secular revolution, withdrew to the country for two years, much to the King´s relief.

He used this brief spell to write some famous works, among them the treatise „De ecclesia - on the church", the paper that would be used against him in his later trial. In essence the treatise is Wiclif reborn. Besides the ugly idea of predestination, to which also Hus subscribed, the demand for a reformed and poor church is upheld. Christ is the head of the church, not a pope who would as well be a sinner or heretic, and who certainly is not infallible.

And above all and everything is the Scripture. The pope may be obeyed only if his dictums are congruent with the teachings of Jesus. The year was 1413.

Meanwhile the church had not only one pope but three, of whom everyone banned his two adversaries and their followers so that the whole of christendom clamoured for an end to this disgracing papal schism and for the start of a true reform of the church. In 1414 therefore a Council was convened at Constance, still the same quiet town on the lake of the same name today. Within the scope of this council especially the secular forces saw an opportunity to reconcile the Wiclifians and Hussites with the church again.

King Waclawas of Bohemia had no children, so the King, later Emperor, Sigismund looked at Bohemia already as his fiefdom, but he wanted a peaceful heritage, free of ecclesiastic strife. It was he, therefore, who assured John Hus a safeconduct to the council, the opportunity of defending his views and the same safeconduct for the return journey, regardless of the outcome. Against the advice of his friends Hus, with a Czech entourage, journeyed confidently to Constance in October 1414.

At first he moved around in Constance unmolested. The council, however, heavily dominated by the Italians, Spaniards, French, English and Germans apparently had no idea to enter into a dispute with the heretical Czech priest. After one hearing and after evaluating his theses, especially in the treatise „De ecclesia", the mirror from which pope and high clergy grimaced upon the world in distorted features, they declared John Hus to be an arch-heretic and put him in irons. Sigismund, to his honour, promptly protested to the Council. He was fed the cool argument that the Council did not feel bound by his guarantee because imperial authority could not infringe on ecclesiastical rights. To his eternal dishonour Sigismund swallowed this insult; he did not want to risk the Council's wrath over the life of a troublesome Czech priest. He needed the church, not the reformer. And so he caved in. Roughly hundred years later an emperor Charles V. expressly ruled out a repetition of this shameful attitude when granting a safeconduct to Luther.

After languishing for seven months in dungeons and irons Hus was led before the Council, chained, for 3 days in June 1415. His spirit, however, was unbroken. He challenged the Council to prove an error of his on the ground of the Scripture. The prelates, however, had not the slightest intention to trade arguments with him and demanded a full recanting; the interpretation of the Scriptures, they maintained, cannot be left to the judgement of an individual but must be reserved for the heads of the church only. Hus was not listening to the many pleas for his retreat, uttered with a last effort of benevolence even by leading Council members, in private. A letter of his was smuggled out of prison and reached Prague:

„Magister John Hus ... greets all faithful Bohemians and prays that they will prevail in God's grace. You should know that the proud, envious, shameful Council has damned my Bohemian books without ever having seen or read them ... they tried to intimidate me but could not prevail over the assistance of the Lord that is in me. They refused to deal with me in written arguments ... I am writing this to you so that you should know that they could not disprove me by the Scriptures or by other proof; they only tried to move me to recant by treachery and threats ... But the good God was with me, is with me and will be with me ... This letter is written on the Wednesday after the name-day of John The Baptist, in dungeon and irons, in the face of death ..."

Sigismund withdrew his last figment of support from Hus when he heard that the Czech priest had also maintained that secular as well as clerical power lose their divine legitimacy if and when their bearers live in mortal sin. Apparently the King remembered something.

On July 6th 1415 the Council of Constance condemned not only Hus, but post mortem also his mentor Wiclif; all their publishings were to be burned. In a bizarre chain of evading murderous responsibility Hus was handed over by King Sigismund to Margrafe Ludwig, the official protector of the Council. This one turned him over to the magistrate of Constance and these worthy gentlemen handed him to the city executioner with the short sentence: „So take magister Johannes Hus and burn him as a heretic". They had the decency, however, to order that he could keep all his clothes and belongings, even his money. So John Hus went to the stake with the ignominious renegade cap, inscribed „arch-heretic" but otherwise fully robed.

He laughed when being led from the dome, where his verdict was read, when he saw the burning of his books going on in the street. He smiled over the peasant who dragged wood to the stake: „Sancta simplicitas!" Before being bound to the stake Hus wanted to speak to the throng of people in German language, but this was thwarted by the Margrafe. They bound him to the stake facing towards West, because a heretic must not see in the direction of the sunrise. When the fire was lit he began to sing: „Jesus Christ, Son of the living God, who had suffered for us, have mercy on me!" After the third repetition, the smoke mercifully suffocated him. (This was taken from the report of the eye-witness Johannes Stumpff).

They took great pains to incinerate every inch of him and his pulverized remains were thrown into the Rhine. A few days later, Wiclif´s body was dug up in Lutterworth and his remains were also thrown into the near river.

This short history would be incomplete if it would not include the fate of Hus´ indefatigable comrade-in-spiritual-arms Hieronymus of Prague. When the Council imprisoned Hus, Hieronymus sped to Constance and started a suicidal campaign of protest there, also by nailing pamphlets on the church and city gates and on the doors of the cardinals´living quarters, demanding an opportunity for a public dispute under a grant of safeconduct. Advised to flee to Bohemia, he was caught on the way and also incarcerated in Constance. In May 1416 he got his opportunity. His eloquence before the Council is on record and he drew a lof of sympathy. He lost it quite as fast, however, when he declared the burning of Hus a crime which God would vindicate. Moreover, he confirmed his belief in the doctrines of Wiclif and Hus. The still impressed Council granted him a recant period of four days, but Hieronymus remained strong. So he was burnt at the stake on May 30th 1416, on the exact spot where his friend left his body eleven months earlier. Also he sang hymns until suffocating.

The courage of both is shining on over the centuries, while the stench of a rotting church still wafts through the corridors of history.

Upon the murder of Hus Bohemia rose like one man, one of the proudest moments of its history; not yet in arms, however. A letter of protest signed by 500 noblemen went to the Council; the signatories declared that Hus´execution was an insult to their nation and that in future only those papal orders were to be followed whose legitimacy was congruent with the Scripture, ultimately to be confirmed by the theological faculty of the Prague university.

The Council responded by ordering the signatories to Constance and the university to be closed. None of that was complied with, of course. After some infighting with King Waclawas, who died over it in 1419, things came to the inevitable stage of events. Sigismund was offered the crown of Bohemia under the condition that he guarantee the so-called „Four Articles of Prague", i.e. communion in both forms (utraque) of bread and wine, no more cronyism in allocating fat-yield clerical posts, free preaching of the Scripture and the sequestering of excess riches owned by priests and monks.

In hindsight it is astonishing that the Bohemian nobility should offer the crown to a king whose cowardly timidity was the cause of death of their new national hero. But Sigismund could not compromise any more; he informed the barons that he expected the unconditional submission of the nation under the church authority. To underline his point he had a Bohemian tried and burnt who propagated the right of the chalice. The victorious pope who had emerged from the Council, Martin V., called for a crusade against the Bohemian heretics and Sigismund marched with an imperial army against Prague in 1420.

Again in one of the finest hours of Czech history the Hussites, as they were called forthwith, engineered a leveé-en-masse and their military leader Jan Ziska drilled the young troops within a matter of weeks into a formidable people´s army. Jan Ziska gave Sigismund battle two times, but with indecisive results. Before the third time a false alarm routed the imperial army all by itself, retreat became a wild flight, Bohemia was free.

Instead of using the moment for clever diplomacy, however, the national army used the occasion to come down on their spiritual adversaries like God´s wrath. In Bohemia, Moravia and Silesia churches and monasteries were pilfered and went up in flames, monks were killed by the hundreds and, since accounts were to be settled at that time already, also a good part of the Germans living in Bohemia. Until 1436 no royal power was exercised in Bohemia any more.

It would lead beyond the scope of this narrative to cover the stages and the tragic end of the Hussitic wars. Let it be enough to say that the movement was ripped apart by insidious infighting of rival faith factions as soon as the common external enemy was eliminated, one of those endless repetitions of history. The interested reader is invited to turn to the historical volumes, preferable so to the volume „The Age of Reformation" by Will Durant, part of his amazing series „The Story of Civilization".

# THE DISCUSSION

W: My first question is: did this church ever vindicate Hus?

B: Vindicate? Never. In 1998, under the Polish pope, the theologian Bruno Forte compiled another criminal history of christianity, called „Instrumentum Laboris" - a work-tool - which became the basic paper of the papal commission. The theme was called „Relations between the church and the crimes of the past". The president of the commission, who else, was Ratzinger, the pope´s alter ego.

W: And, the results?

B: They were not published. Insiders however speculate that the zealous monk Savonarola might be beatified, Hus would be acknowledged as an eminent spirit, but with Giordano Bruno there will be only a nod of regret for having killed him. On the whole, the findings of the commission are meant to become part of a millenium address, where „the guilt of the sons and daughters of the church" will be deplored, but never the miserable failing of a miserable institution. And, so may I add: what daughters, please?

W: So no admission of guilt, even now?

B: This Roman Catholic church has become a prisoner of its own. How can this church be „holy" in its own hyperbolic meaning if she has to confess to have sinned, not only against mankind but against the Spirit whom she declares to possess exclusively? Moreover, do not forget that the reformers are a minority in this body yet. The orthodox majority is stemming itself against the tide with the - objectively correct - argument that self-flagellation would only serve the enemies of their organization. So: regret yes, sin - none. Moreover, no one would believe in the morals of the institution afterwards.

W: To hell with her!

B: So be it. But all this has us led away from Hus. His conduct has reserved him a front place in history, no doubt. But was he also a tool of evolution?

W: I thougt about it many times but I came not to a conclusion as yet. The main argument against it is that he and his followers kept adhering to the callous idea of pre-determination, just as their mentor Wiclif was tied to his Augustine, and he, in turn, to Paul. In my opinion no one of the thinkers who condone pre-determination can be part of evolution because she is the exact opposite of it. Within pre-determination there is no room for evolution; precisely said, evolution is the arch-enemy of pre-determination. On this count Hus failed completely.

B: We always have to consider that also at his time there was no concept of evolution, neither in the natural sciences nor in philosophy. Again were are back to the point where we have to raise the legal shield: no one can be accused of violation of a law before the onset of the law, no?

W: No! Your idea would reduce the issue to pure formalism. The message through Yeshua was loud and clear: The free will of man is called upon and will ultimately shape his attitude towards the Divine Spirit. It shall not be overpowered nor shall it be neglected by the revelation. The real culprits are Paul & Co. They abolished free will and substituted it by a scenario without escape. Repulsive enough if it is believed individually, but murderous in the moment where an organization is ramming it through mercilessly.

B: Another plus for poor Hus; he never knew it better, was raised in this shamanism?

W: I am sorry to reject this idea also. Hus knew the four reports on Yeshua by heart and had read the Greek philosophers. Fact is that his eminent mind did not dare to tell Paul and Augustine that they were diminishing us to puppets on a string.

B: Don´t you think that they would have burnt him all the sooner for this?

W: Evidently so, but then he would have died for a truly worthy cause.

B: Slow now, slow, my friend! You mean that he died for a trifling cause?

W: Not in his opinion. Let us call them minor causes compared to the abolition of pre-determination. Just as a hundred years later Martin Luther dared his life for many legitimate but ultimately secondary values.

B: Such as?

W: The notion of a Eucharist, dominance by a scandalized Vatican, the confessional, doing away with Mariolatry ...

B: But you forgot a very primary value he advocated: the direct access of the believer to his God, drawing justification from a personal belief in him?

W: Let us reserve that for our discussion on him, will you? What is counting here is that anybody who advocates pre-determination is an obstacle in the path of evolution. Luther did not follow Wiclif and Hus here, and we praise him for that.

B: Let us be fair. In essence you are saying that nobody who accepts pre-determination can be part of the evolution of mind, isn´t it?

W: This is exactly what I mean, yes.

B: At this point I come in under your guard: you are underrating evolution. You are binding her non-existence to a single human article of belief, unpalatable as it may be. And stopped by that she waits until this mental barricade has come down in all people and only then she gets moving again.

Forgive me to say so but you are degrading evolution to something three-dimensional and solid that could be upheld by a roadblock that some zealot erected?

(B): No sir! She is flowing around it like a tide, onwards, around many of this kind, knowing that their shaky fundaments will crumble sooner or later. Pre-determination is only one of them, and until this and other stone-age notions are washed away finally she is working already a thousand miles beyond, always doing away with the minor obstacles first, simply because they are easier to overcome. But the major ones are not forgotten, it just takes longer to eradicate them from the minds of our race.

You are denying Hus an evolutionary status because he held fast to an obsolete concept, of which he was very much convinced. Would you at least agree with me that he helped to tear down quite a few minor ones?

W: I cannot help but to say that the introduction of the Eucharist also in liquid form is not an evolutionary notion. On the contrary; to go to war because of this is just plain folly.

B: The Hussite wars were not fought over this issue alone, nor mainly.

W: Well, we have read this in the historical part of this chapter. This reduces his contribution to evolution in lashing out against the sale of indulgences, attacking the morals of the clergy, denouncing the pope as antichrist - but he did not kick at the notion of a church as such, one to be run by priests and laymen on equal rights - or without professional priests, preferably so.

B: And why not? Because he felt very much as a part of the system, you wanted to say, no? Here we are at another point, my friend. The „minor" issues, as you call them, were formidable major reasons for him to risk his life. Probably they were high enough hills to block his view and those of his contemporaries to the mountains of fundamental abuse of the revelation through Yeshua. Will you hold this against him, or them?

W: Certainly not, I bow before his personal courage, above all to his serene, almost humorous attitude in his last minutes here.

B: We are coming to an ultimate point now: you are of the debatable opinion that Hus did not do enough for the evolution of mind during his lifetime. Would you agree with me if I say that, at any rate, his behaviour in the face of death was truly evolutionary?

W: To this I fully subscribe, yes.

B: There you see? Perhaps you cannot accept that the live Hus was a blockbuster for evolution, but surely his death was a semen of her for many a fertile mind thereafter - and where is the difference now?

W: The difference is that only a war sprang from this seed, to be ended in disaster and shame.

B: I think that again you are underestimating evolution. The decade after his death means very little to her. The centuries - much more so. The mere fact that we, today, are questioning the system of priest churches openly, without getting burnt by them, is also an evolutionary progress to which Hus contributed - in life and death.

W: What shall we write on his epitaph?

B: E cinere evolutio - from the ashes, evolution.

# MARTIN LUTHER

**1483 - 1546**

# THE MAN

Martin Luther was born on November 10th 1483 in Eisleben. His father, Hans Luther, was a smallholder, later became a miner in Mansfeld. Martin´s childhood was anything but a dream. His father was an unforgiving man who beat Martin mercilessly for any small trespasses. His mother was hardly kinder to him, perhaps in awe of her husband, and whipped him for trifles. Martin did not come to receive love until he married. It is astonishing that Martin could become a kind and caring father to his children, carrying this mortgage with him. But, by some quirk of history, without this sinister upbringing he probably would not have become a monk first, as he later admitted.

The beating went on at school, in Mansfeld and in Magdeburg. Only when he could move in as a boarder to Mrs. Cotta in Eisenach he experienced for the first time three years of happiness; he was 14 by then.

When he was 18 his father sent him to the university of Erfurt, to study philosophy and theology. With 22 years he graduated to Magister - and left theology, in his opinion forever. He took up the study of law, much to the pleasure of his father, who, with all his Old Testament behaviour, was fiercely anticlerical. But hardly had two months passed when he received the message from Martin that he would enter a monastery. What happened?

Every schoolboy today knows the outward story, the lightning which struck into a near tree during a thunderstorm when he was wandering back to Erfurt after a visit to his parents. It would be downright silly to infer that in the seconds thereafter Martin offered a bargain to God: spare my life and I shall become a monk. The reasons were far deeper and the lightning episode was evidently the opener for a torrent that had built up in him over the recent years, a torrent of guilt.

It would be inconceivable that his childhood would not leave its scars in his consciousness. The Jahve-father who avenged also minor sins without mercy was always looming formidably in the background, condemning not only the sins of the flesh but killing also pure, natural joy. The fire and brimstone images of hell which his mother warningly fed him - all this was the basso continuo on which the melody of life had to be written, severe, austere, hardworking and without any dandelions.

Martin, in his student years at Erfurt, wrote lighter melodies. Puberty saw him as a healthy, joyous fellow who probably also participated in some heavy drinking bouts for which the students were famous. But the well had been poisoned thoroughly already. Sex, joy and harmless trivia were only machinations of the Satan, he came to realize in his torn mind. Reading the joyless Paul and Augustine probably aggravated his fear of sin - and hell - so that also harmless pastimes were building up guilt upon guilt in him. Also without any lightning this bow, pulled ever tighter, would have snapped sooner or later. He was longing for peace of mind, redemption, a heaven where he was safe from the assaults of Satan. A monastery was the logical choice for a battered, twisted mind. Yahve had caught up with him.

And stayed with him for quite some time. Martin castigated himself mercilessly to expel the devil from his young body, until the inevitable breakdown. His superior and fellow novices succeded to soften him. The Vicar of the Augustine monks had a different notion in mind when he advised him to study the works of Augustine. To Martin´s eternal credit he found the concept of pre-destination unsavory already then, which Augustine drew from Paul. „Justification by belief" took form in him already then and there.

In 1508 Martin Luther was transferred to the Wittenberg monastery and given a lectorate for physics and logics at the university there, later on the chair of theology.

Two years later his order sent him on a mission to Rome where he underwent with a glowing heart all the motions prescribed for pilgrims in order to win a lasting supply of indulgences.

He did not move in high circles there so it can safely be assumed that he learned of the sybaritic life in the Vatican by hearsay only. This, however, did not refrain him in later years to lambast the Rome of 1510 with his usual caustic fervour.

In 1511 he was promoted to Vicar General of the order´s province but kept preaching in the Wittenberg church. Gradually he began to recognize the depravity of the clergy, something that he had read before in a treatise of Hus which miraculously had survived in his Erfurt monastery and which made him develop serious doubts on the wisdom of the official church already then.

His conviction that man can be justified in and through belief crystallized over the years ever more. When preaching on it in Dresden in July 1517, however, the Saxonian Duke George took offence. Raising belief over virtue, he lectured the monk, would only make the people more adamant and rebellious.

It was the bankers who, unwittingly so, supplied Luther with his platform to history. Prince Albrecht of Brandenburg had to pay some 20.000 guilders to the Vatican coffers for his nomination as Prince Archbishop of Mainz. Saving the burghers who had been tithed that way two times already during the past ten years for two new bishops the nobleman turned to the wealthy Fuggers who advanced the sum. Albrecht was allowed by Pope Leo X. to sell indulgences for finishing the works in progress with the new Basilica in Rome.

The Fugger loan was to be repaid by the income from the indulgence sales first, only the surplus would find its way to Rome. Wary as bankers have been at all times the sales preacher groups were each accompanied by a Fugger representative who held one key to the strongbox.

One of the best salesmen-monks was the Dominican John Tetzel. In best sales-wagon style he did not try to mince words but convinced his congregations that a terrific bargain was waiting for them: indulgence not only for past sins but also for all future ones, in other words a certified ticket to heaven. The money poured in.

The now Duke Frederic of Saxonia, however, had no mind to see Saxonian money emigrating to Rome and forbade the indulgence preachings within his territory. Tetzel, ever the wily salesman, tried to sidestep this embargo by preaching in communities close to Saxonia´s border and, of course, drew crowds over it, also from Wittenberg. Upon return, some showed their documents to professor Luther, asking him to validate it. Luther, however, rejected any confirmation. When Tetzel heard of it he lashed out against him in a way which Luther could not take lying down. He had awakened the lion.

His rebuttal were the famous 95 theses which he nailed, in the customary academic tradition, to the portal of the Wittenberg church. They were in Latin but he had copies made in the vernacular which were distributed to the people; one he sent with a letter of due deference to Prince-Archbishop Albrecht of Mainz.

The devout catholic Luther had not the least idea at that time to rip into the church organization. All theses centered around the misuse and inconsistencies of the indulgences only.

Apparently also Luther had a good market sense. The multitude of indulgences, so ran one of his arguments, is bringing down the „market", a word he never used, of course; it diminishes the preparedness of the individual to refrain from sin and degrades the indulgence documents to a paper currency by which everyone could buy eternal insurance. He did not - yet - assail the prerogatives of the Pope who claimed to hold the keys to purgatory exclusively. Without realizing it he had trod loose an avalanche.

The temperature rose steeply. Tetzel, never to be bested, answered with 106 anti-theses. A salesman of his who tried to peddle them in Wittenberg was beaten up by students and his total supply was set to flames. Again Luther retaliated with another treatise. But things were not any more a debate between monks; they had become the topic of the day in many cities all over Germany. Apparently Luther had spoken for thousands, burghers and nobility alike; the anti-Rome faction also among the lower clergy had grown in the decades before, thanks to an Alexander VI. and Julius II.

The orthodox clergy, however, was not slow to respond. From Cologne the inquisitor van Hoogstraaten beckoned with the stake. The Vice Chancellor of the Ingolstadt university, John Eck, accused Luther of spreading Hussite ideas. Luther´s fighting instincts prompted him to release yet another paper, called „Resolutiones", in April 1518. One exemplar of it he sent to Pope Leo X. with a letter that expressed total obedience and loyalty, setting him off favorably against his predecessors.

Under all this amiability and deference, however, the Pope smelled high treason, because Luther put the councils over the Pope, disputed the power of canonized saints and, above all, sailed into the basic concept and practice of indulgences.

The curia might have forgiven Luther the theological aberrations, but never his frontal attack against the indulgences which were the main source of income for a sybaritic, pompous and warfaring Vatican. So a papal summons went out to Luther to appear in Rome.

Luther turned to his Duke Frederic of Saxonia to gain protection against extradition to Rome, which was granted. Also the Emperor Maximilian who was at loggerheads with the Vatican sent a note to the Duke to extend „great care to this monk".

Just at that time sentiments ran high in Germany against the Pope who had proposed to the Emperor to levy a new tax in Germany for another crusade against the Turks, something to be decided by the Reichstag in Augsburg in 1518. The assembly not only rejected this demand but added a lot of caveats for the future dealings of the Vatican, especially as to the confirmation fees payable for newly appointed prelates, fees for the Roman Court proceedings and recriminations against the bestowing of vacant sees in Germany to Italian priests.

The Medici Leo X. took this flat rejection with remarkable good grace, he was not ruthless like Alexander VI. nor as combative as Julius II. While the assembly was still proceeding Luther´s summons to Rome was withdrawn, surely meant as a tranquilizer towards the Germans. Instead, Luther was ordered to appear before the papal delegate at the Reichstag, Cardinal Cajetan. The accusation cited disobedience and heresy. The Pope instructed his delegate to imprison Luther and to extradite him to Rome in case he would not recant.

Maximilian, however, issued an imperial safe-conduct to Luther, who considered him to be more trustworthy than a Sigismund V..

So Luther appeared before Cajetan from the 12th to 14th of October 1518 in Augsburg.

The papal delegate had no mind to trade theological arguments with him. He simply demanded a recantation and Luther´s pledge not to attack the church organization again. Luther, whose hopes of explaining his case were aborted, refused. Cajetan turned to Duke Frederic to have him sent to Rome, which Frederic promptly refused. This time the safe-conduct worked; Luther returned to Wittenberg with the intention to wage war with the Antichrist in Rome from now on.

Leo X., still the noble Medici, sent Frederic the Golden Rose, the highest Vatican decoration. His messenger Miltitz was instructed to convince the Duke to silence Luther peacefully, in the larger interests of the church. To his surprise Miltitz found Germany in the middle of an anti-papal uproar. He instantly dismissed the super-salesmonk Tetzel and accused him of embezzlement; Tetzel retired into his monastery and died the next year, hardly consoled by a letter from Luther who told him not to worry, because „this child has a totally different father, not you".

Luther was not fighting alone any more, though. Eminent humanists rallied around him, Melanchthon, Karlstadt, Erasmus of Rotterdam. When the orthodox Eck demanded a disputation with Karlstadt in Leipzig, a town that was openly hostile to the new ideas, Luther joined him. While Karstadt was the loser against the eloquent Eck, Luther gave him battle for two days. The wily Eck correctly suspected that Luther had much more in store than he had put forward until now and he succeeded that Luther, in the heat of battle, came out openly on the primate of the Roman bishops.

Eck retorted that this was unabashed Hussite creed, whereupon Luther told the audience that also councils can err and that Hus had developed many a good doctrine.

In the end this was all Eck wanted to hear and to be witnessed. Eck demanded Luther´s excommunication, but Leo X. apparently had no information on how really deep Lutheran thinking was already anchored in Germany - and stalled. The Medici diplomat was still hopeful that the issue could be resolved in a consensus with the German dukes.

The humanists around Luther, especially so Ulrich von Hutten, continued their attacks on the Vatican. Luther also poured oil on the fire by a treatise in the spring of 1520 where he for the first time dealt openly with „the Sodom in Rome, the teachers of destruction who are undermining the church of God and wash their hands in our blood ...".

Even a cultivated Medici could not ignore this declaration of war. Leo X. issued the famous bulla „Exsurge Domine" on June 15th 1520. In it, fortyone theses of Luther were declared heretic. If he would not recant within 60 days he would be declared anathema and wherever he lived the interdict would be spelled over the community. The war was on.

Luther used the 60 days to write and publish - in German language - his famous treatise „To the christian nobility of German nation and on the improvement of the christian Estate". He called upon the German clergy to form a German national church under the leadership of Prince-Archbishop Albrecht of Mainz. The number of begging orders should be drastically reduced. Marriage should be allowed to priests. Final vows for monks and nuns should be allowed only for those over the age of thirty. The German church must find a reconciliation with the Hussites. In quoting the bulla´s initial words he ends: „O Christ, my Lord, rise up, let dawn your judgement day and smash the devil in Rome!"

The sensation in Germany was perfect, the printing presses went hot in reproducing the treatise. Luther had not only lashed out against a rotten church but had struck a national nerve as well.

In September 1520 the tireless Eck published the excommunication bulla in Germany. Luther fired back with his second manifesto „On the Babylonian captivity of the church" and, shortly after, his third: „Of the freedom of christian man". The tide had turned already. Eck was chased out of most cities where he presented the excommunication bulla. On December 10th 1520 Luther burnt the bulla publicly before a city gate of Wittenberg.

For good measure Luther declared on the next day that without discarding papal dogmas first nobody could hope to reach the kingdom of heavens. As Durant aptly comments: the monk had excommunicated the Pope.

Inevitably, politics entered the scene. The king of Spain, later emperor Charles V. was a devout catholic and reigned over Spanish catholics who would never tolerate a ruler who was benign to heretics. On the other hand he had consented to the demand of the German Princes that German nationals could only be tried before ordinary German courts.

When he called for another Reichstag in Worms in 1521 he did so for political reasons only, not because of Luther. He needed the support of a functioning Holy Roman Empire for his claim to Milan, which was contested by the French, and for saving Hungary from the Turks. He was well aware that the Empire and the church needed each other; the ruin of one would also be the undoing of the other. His line was quite clear therefore: the Lutheran movement had to be silenced, quickly.

Contrary to his belief the Reichstag knew hardly any other topic but Luther´s ideas. When Cardinal Alexander demanded the immediate sentencing of Luther, the assembly stalled and called for a hearing. So Luther was summoned to Worms, again under an imperial safe-conduct. To his honour, Charles V. stuck to his word inspite of massive interventions by the curia to extradite Luther.

On the first day, April 17th, Luther was overwhelmed by the pageantry displayed by the assembly. When his scripts were shown to him and he was commanded to recant, he asked for 24 hours of time, which was granted. On the next day, before a packed audience, Luther parried the exhortation to recant by maintaining that his statements on the rampant abuse in the church were publicly shared. As to theology he declared - like Hus - that he would recant anything that would disprove him by the scriptures.

When his accuser John von der Ecken confronted him with the remark that in the dogmas issued by the councils there is no error, Luther replied: „Well there are errors, and I shall prove it". This was too much for the Emperor who terminated the scene with a terse „We do not want to hear any more since it is evident now that Luther refutes the councils".

The next day Charles V. wanted the German Princes to sign a document of loyalty, pledging their efforts to eradicate Luther´s heresies. „... a single monk who attacks thousand years of christianity simply cannot be right". Four Princes signed, but not Frederic of Saxonia nor Ludwig of the Palatinate. But the emperor kept his promise, Luther could start his journey back to Wittenberg on April 26th. But Frederic, who surmised that after the expiry of the safe-conduct on May 6th Luther could be kidnapped by the Emperor´s militia, spirited him away under a faked ambush to the Wartburg over Eisenach.

On May 6th the Emperor submitted to the Reichstag the „Edict of Worms" putting Luther under the imperial ban. Two days later Pope Leo X. changes sides in the dispute over Milan - from the French king to Charles V.

From May 1521 to February 1522 Luther sat in the Wartburg, wearing nobleman´s garb, biding his time but also translating the bible into German, while Germany saw anticlerical revolts in a thousand places, many of them violent. In March 1522 he slipped out from the Wartburg to prevent violence in his home town of Wittenberg, successfully so. The monasteries there and elsewhere emptied peacefully, Latin mass was abolished, the Eucharist was passed out „utraque", veneration of Mary was ridiculed.

Luther resumed his activities as professor and parish priest in Wittenberg; Duke Frederic paid him a modest annual salary. His German bible was a tremendous success, also forming the German language for centuries, and while the publishers earned a fortune with it he received not a penny of royalties. Instead, he set out to formulate his theology precisely now.

The bible, Old and New Testament, he accpeted as a divine revelation, the infallible word of God. He made short shrift of reason; this, he said, is the greatest enemy of belief, the devil´s whore. In the same way he dealt with scholastic thinking; christian faith cannot be proven by rational thinking. Therefore, he demanded, do away with the books of this treacherous, conceited, damned pagan Aristoteles.

He made no compromise in the litteral interpretation of the Bible, however, both parts. He lectured Erasmus and other humanists fiercely on their allegoric interpretation of the bible, calling it just another form of atheism. The bible for him was not a product of human intelligence but a gift from heaven. Finis.

First Luther wanted to reform the church and then, inevitably, theology. Involved in this he realized too late that his New Order could not be confined to these fields but would be embraced by all wordly suppressed, in the first line by the impoverished serfs of secular and clerical aristocracy, the peasants. There had been dozens of peasant uprisings before him, but being of local spontaneous nature and missing ideology they were easily and cruelly suppressed.

Now, however, that the „German Nightingale" had started to sing the movement found that it had a spiritual basis all along, in the vernacular which they could understand and interprete. The peasant wars from 1524-26 sprang up in Southern Germany and quickly won knights as leaders who knew warfare well, Sickingen, Berlichingen and the mercenary leader Geyer. As with so many promising uprisings, however, they failed to unite under a central command.

In March 1525 a convent of peasant delegates formulated the famous „Twelve Articles" of Memmingen, whom they also sent to Luther, asking for his assistance. In his response „Exhortation For Peace" Luther tried to find a formula that would, on one side, stop the murderous rioting, on the other he conceded that the peasants had a just cause for a redress of their pariah treatment by their lords.

His main concern was that violence would only damage the religious reform. Pulling back from his treatise „Of The Freedom Of Christian Man" he preached Paul to the peasants whereas any Government is ordained by God and that spiritual freedom is very well compatible with serfdom, even slavery.

As could be expected he convinced neither side. The aristocracy accused him of clandestine cooperation with the revolutionaries, whereas these had no more mind for subtle theology.

They wanted to be freed of tithes, secular taxes, unpaid labor, the hunting of the migthy over tilled land and most of all to be freed from hunger and squalor.

So the armies went to the field and in almost all parts of Germany peasant hordes plundered and burnt monasteries and castles, from the Rhine to Southern Tyrolia. The tales of the atrocities committed reached Luther who quickly penned the pamphlet „Against the plundering and murdering hordes of peasants".

In it, he pulled out all stops of mercy, taking clearly the side of the lords and prelates. He was acutely aware of the open or tacit accusations that his teachings had kindled the uprising and that further inflammation, or a victory of the peasant side, could well be the end of his road. It could be also that the pragmatist in him foresaw the strategic outcome of the revolt: Able but split forces on one side, highly motivated, poorly trained and above all not coordinated. On the other disciplined and trained cadres and mercenaries, able leaders like George Truchsess of Hohenlohe - and his artillery, not to forget.

Whatever Luther´s rationale may have been, his pamphlet advocated to „smash, strangle and stab (the rebellious peasants) because nothing is more poisonous, damaging or diabolical than a rebel who should be clubbed to death like a rabid dog ..."

The end is known to all. At the end of 1526 the uprising was drowned in a sea of blood. More than 100.000 peasants lost their life in battle, tens of thousands, houses burnt, roamed in the woods or formed robber gangs. Around 20.000 were executed.

Only the Thirty Years´War surpassed the loss of human life and property that were caused by the peasant uprising.

Also Luther can be counted under the victims of the peasant war. Charles V. was quick to denounce the uprising as a „Lutheran movement", not admitting in his Habsburg haughtiness that it was a socially driven act of utter despair.

When the smoke of the ruins and the smell of rotten bodies had cleared away Luther showed no remorse nor pity. He knew that his New Order had just barely escaped the loss of credibility and that it must gain new ground with the Dukedoms, independent cities and within the lower clergy who had protected him in Wittenberg, Augsburg and Worms. They, in turn, decided to overlook the remark he had made a few years earlier that he would welcome an uprising, even when washing hands in the blood of prelates.

A growing creed brings growing power, spiritually and wordly, and power has always had the danger of corrupting those who wield it. Luther was no exception to that. After the peasant uprising and some local governments of religious fanatics had been quelled his position was more prominent and commanding than ever. In the following years one could observe, however, a growing intolerance and a trend to dogmas in him, accompanied by a language that was far more Yahve than Christ.

The first to suffer from this were the Jews. Until about 1537 Luther saw them not so much as the murderers of Yeshua but was of the opinion that „... if they are treated friendly and if one teaches them from the Holy Scripture a great many of them should become good christians ...“ Since Luther also believed in the letter of the Old Testament, he expected them to connect in time to protestantism. He overlooked, however, that the New Testament would have to be part of the bargain also, something to which no orthodox Jew would consent.

Disappointment over this grew into uncontrolled rage over the years. He ended up to see the Jews and papists as one common enemy, „two pants made from one cloth“. From private dinner talks where he found no opponents he went to print in a language that is to his eternal shame and which was the welcome quarry for all antisemites of later centuries: „Burn their synagogues, destroy their houses, take away from them all books and scripts, forbid their rabbis to preach upon penalty of death, shove them off the street, forbid their usury, confiscate their cash and gold, and, if all this will not help, chase them away like rabid dogs“. Small wonder that Hitler was glad to oblige, if for completely different but not less fanatic reasons.

Apart from this stain which he inflicted on himself was his growing intransigence to critical opinions upon his teachings, not accepting „... you or an angel from heaven to be a judge over my teachings and ... whoever does not accept my teaching he may not enter heaven“.

In the first line this final language was directed at the protestant sects which sprang up everywhere; most have lasted unto our times. History had caught up with Luther. Just as the early christian church had to fight off its heretics so protestantism had no choice but to do likewise, putting its very existence and the common good over individual faith.

So he lashed out against Ana-Baptists and Zwinglians, condemning above all the notion of an equal distribution of wordly goods. He knew very well that his creed would receive support from burghers and princes only if this idea would not spread.

So again, in best Yahve style, he advocated to the Governments in 1530 „... to level the death penalty on all supporters of wealth-sharing or against teachers who preach against an article of faith ...“ Sebastian Franck commented that more freedom of speech and faith could be found among the Turks than in the protestant states of his time.

Consequently Luther´s time saw already the first martyrs, some of them condemned to death by a court over which - of all persons - Melanchthon presided. It was Luther who condoned the expulsion of catholics from protestant dukedoms. The magistrates of Augsburg or Frankfurt ordered all those out of the city who would not convert to protestantism within eight days (1537). Books contrary or critical to the new creed were indexed. And, in an irony of history, anathema was decreed on all who questioned a basic tenet of the New Faith.

It is reported that in his final years Luther found a more forgiving stance towards Jews and dissidents. The mellowness of age however could not repair the damage that was done, disfiguring the New Order and poisoning the political and religious climate of the next centuries.

In this short presentation, however, Luther should not go down only as the ogre who finally made a travesty of his reforms.

His fiery and courageous mind was needed to pry loose a much-needed reform.

His scathing rhetoric in the vernacular was indispensable to drive his ideas home.

His siding with the established powers during the peasant war was an act of survival, not of his, but of the new creed.

Pity is that he could not tolerate opposition. So instead of becoming the venerable elder statesman of a new religion he ended up much like another Pope.

He died on February 18th 1546, the most venerated and cursed person of his century.

# THE DISCUSSION

B: When reading this fragment of history which we have digested mostly from our beloved Will Durant I am asking myself whether we have done justice to the man?

W: Not nearly. But would it have made a difference if we had used fifty or five hundred pages of learned Lutheran biography? I certainly wish that our readers would sit down with Durant and listen to his compelling narrative of this man and his times. Trouble is, we have too many data on Martin Luther, he is the best documented man in all religious history, thanks to the printing press that was invented in his time. I am quite aware of our torso and feel very humble, inspite of all our daring.

B: So I am asking in all humbleness: was Luther a promoter of evolution or not?

W: In my opinion, by all means.

B: In my opinion, by not all means.

W: Would you care to explain that?

B: „By all means" represents a total claim, including all his thoughts and all his writings. To this I cannot agree. What we have seen in our minimized curriculum is enough to attribute grey, even black shades to an evolutionary painting of him.

W: What do you prefer, to look at the warts in a face or to let the whole face impress you?

B: Certainly I do not prefer warts. But just as certainly I maintain that they are disfiguring, if not distorting a face. I do not prefer to look at the grey or black shades in Martin Luther´s portrait. I look at him as a whole: youth, monk, reformer, loving husband and father, politician, spiritus rector, shining lance and tainted bludgeon - he was all of it.

W: By all means.

B: Now your wording has a different ring.

W: I know. You resented it in the context of his contribution to evolution. But I think that we cannot go about our discussion like accountants: this of him to the credit side, this to the debit and when we draw the balance we see a plus or minus. Not so. Luther's shortcomings are manifest, even in our nutshell biography. My proposal is that we leave them out altogether and concentrate on his ideas and doings that were evolutionary in our opinion. What about that?

B: We have no other choice, isn't it?

W: Then I shall start. His fight against the sale of indulgences, later on with the whole church apparatus is a progress for evolution. For the first time since the early councils an individual stood up against the formidable machine of councils, canonized saints and Popes to tell them that they had outlived their purpose, made a travesty of the organization and, still worse, of the revelation through Yeshua. If the Saxonian Duke would not have been his John of Gaunt he would have ended on the stake just as Hus did.

B: No doubt. But is it enough to hold a mirror to the face of a corrupt church? He did not want to abolish it, at least not in his early time. This, for me, would have been truly evolutionary.

W: Patience, please. He arrived at this solution only a little bit later, when he saw that a church reform, top to bottom, was impossible.

B: But he hever questioned the unholy alliance of throne and altar. Much more so, he based his new church on the same principle.

W: Would the new religion have had any chance by not doing so? What you are doing is to look to the desirable goals of evolution in our times, where a faith can emerge that is based not on churches or priests - let alone governments - but on all followers, with equal rights. To Luther this idea never occurred. He saw a clear leadership principle, but devoid of absolute rule. For him this was a daring enough concept, and very evolutionary for his times.

B:  I agree, I was asking too much of him. But I am justified to ask if his partial success was indeed a stepping stone to a new plateau of the evolution of consciousness?

W:  In my opinion it was not only a stepping stone but the new plateau itself. Until him the so-called christian faith was administered by a clique of misguided rulers who fed portions of the faith to so many beggars at will. They claimed old tenets that outside of the organization was not only void space, but the realm of the devil. So they doled out their so-called sacraments in well calculated portions to keep their faithful in despondency.

Their fear and hate was understandable when Luther brandished in their face his conviction that every christian is his own priest before God and that the justification of man is based on his individual belief in him. For me, that was - and is - a unique vision that lifted the fog from yet another plateau of the evolution of human consciousness.

B:  It is, no doubt. It is all the more compelling because at the same time he did away with pre-determination, this arch-enemy of evolution. Some sinister sects which sprang up in his wake still cling to it, it cannot be held against him. In my opinion it is this accomplishment that rates highest on an evolutionary count.

W:  No, only combined they do. When the individual dares to stand alone before his Creator it makes sense only if he or she is not programmed since the beginning of the creation, but has made his/her choice in free will.

B:  It is thrilling to see Luther analyzing Paul who held the opposite view. But he readily drew from him the spiritual basis for his „The just lives by his faith“?

W:  This is not the only inconsistency in his relations with Paul. In condemning the riotous peasants he invoked him again by upholding that each government is God-ordained. To uphold law and order and above all to save the new creed he told them that the inward freedom is enough, even if the outward is withheld.

B: We are gliding to the debit side of Luther, which we ruled out. Is there any other contribution to evolution besides these we mentioned?

W: Monumental as they are, there is hardly any need for others. One more, perhaps. In his teachings he made no difference at all between the role of man or woman before God. On the contrary he saw women on a par with men, waving goodbye to the homophile Aristotle and the asisine scholastics. His married life is the best proof thereof. From then onward women certainly were not „liberated" in today´s meaning but clearly raised to equal status with men before the Creator.

B: I fully agree, also this was an important contribution to the evolution of consciousness. But, forgive me, I cannot help it: also protestant regimes burnt witches, no?

W: Luther actively believed in demons and witches, yes, as any man or woman of his time, educated or not. But he never advocated inquisition. So this cannot be held against him nor any other crimes against humanity that were perpetrated by protestant or by the counter-reformist regimes later.

B: Or the holocaust in the 20th century?

W: Of course we are in the dark side of the man´s painting here, fully. Let us state clearly that his tirades against the Jews eased the way to anti-semitism in the next centuries. But Luther was only used as a pretext by the murderous crowds or regimes afterwards, be it greed, sadism or notions of racial superiority -

B: - or religion?

W: The churches condoned it, alas, up to Hitler, or looked the other way, but they never started all-out persecution. This has to be kept in mind. The stain on Luther is there, clearly, and will not be washed away.

B: And how about our concept of the heretic who shows unity of thought and deed in his life?

W: You are invoking the old Donatist notion that only a sinless priest can hand out valid sacraments? With Luther you have the best example that this notorious idea is absurd. He was not newly consecrating the sheeps in his flock but flung the gate wide open: „graze cheerfully as individuals!" By that he brought back an element in the faith to a Creator that Paul & Co. had absconded apparently forever: the wild and burning joy that God is, God cares for and God responds to the individual directly. This, in my humble opinion, is the major contribution of Luther to the evolution of our minds.

B: Well spoken. What are we writing on his epitaph?

W: He said it already in his lifetime: „Here I stand, I cannot do otherwise, God help me!"

# GIORDANO BRUNO

## 1548 - 1600

# THE MAN

When Giordano Bruno was burnt on the Piazza Campo degli Fiori -
of all names - on February 19th 1600 he had lived for 52 years, the
last 8 thereof in the dungeons of the inquisition in Venice and
Rome. But before and while his body rotted in chains his mind had
soared into the cosmos and into infinity, preempting today's
cosmology and relativity. He had found God everywhere and in all
things. Was he burnt alive for that? We shall see.

He entered this world in 1548 in Nola, near Naples. We do not
know anything about his childhood and also he, a prolific writer, left
no autobiographic material. History meets him again only when he
entered the monastery of the Dominicans in Naples at the age of
seventeen, for motives unknown. He changed his first name from
Filippo to Giordano.

The library of the monastery offered a heady wine by books not
only on theology but also on great thinkers like Democrit, Epikur,
Lucrez, Platon and Aristoteles as a Thomasian „must", the great
islamic writers Ibn Sina, Averroes and the Jewish philosopher Ibn
Gebirol. Most of all he was caught by the visions of the (Cardinal)
Nicolaus of Cues who had lived a hundred years before him.
Nicolaus already saw an infinite universe, certainly not our earth as
the center of it and God not being „in" it but „being it". We do not
know whether Baruch Spinoza had read him also or whether he
came to the identical vision all by himself.

The young monk Giordano traded Aristotle, the Scholastics and
especially the founder of the order, Thomas Aquinas, very readily
for the other names we have mentioned - but not overtly, of course.
For a Neapolitan his sexual awakening must have come late
because he was ordained a priest in 1572 at the age of 24 - and
started to have sincere doubts on a Trinity, Eucharist and other
dogmas only afterwards - why, we do not know.

He was lectured twice very sternly by his superiors probably
because he discussed his doubts with his fellow monks in the old
Italian penchant for talk. His superiors may have viewed him as a
potential danger for the unwitting minds. Inevitably Giordano

decided to quit priesthood and monastery in 1576, wore civilian clothes, called himself Filippo again and worked as a teacher in a school in Noli near Genua. Quite foreseeably so this activity could not fill his restless mind.

After only four months of teaching he wandered over the Alps, most of the time in a monk´s tunic because this secured food and a dry room with the monasteries on the way. He ended his journey in Geneva where he soon clashed with the Calvinist hierarchy when he pointed out a list of errors in a lecture by a Calvinist theologian. Already at this time he must have had a fine gift of dialectics because the Consistorium acquitted him. Bruno knew that his luck would not hold for a second time and retreated into France, Toulouse. There he subsisted for a year and a half by lecturing on his despised Aristotle, especially on „De anima". He was wise enough not to tell the university of his true feelings on Aristotle and the Scholastics.

1581 he went to Paris. Bruno had acquired more fame with his mnemotechnics than with his philosophy; the talk of his brilliant memory came before King Henry III. who summoned him and was impressed. Bruno taught his memorizing technique to the King who awarded him the post of professor on the Collège de France. If Bruno had had other blood than Neapolitan he would have rested on this sinecure for a lifetime - which of course he did not. Instead he wrote a comedy called „Il candelaio - the torchbearer" in which he ridiculed the clergy and his fellow professors. Feelings towards him cooled immediately so he thought it wise to change station again. This time he went to England, equipped with a letter of recommendation by the grateful King to his ambassador in London, Michel de Castelnau. This nobleman offered him lodging and boarding on his country estate so that Bruno found time to write some of his outstanding treatises. Moreover, there he met and conversed with some of the most brilliant minds of England such as the Earl of Leicester, Edmund Spenser, Gabriel Harvey and others. His connection enabled him also to be received by Queen Elisabeth. His favourable comments on the Great Queen, who was anathema to Emperor Philip and the whole catholic church, were part of the later indiction against him by the inquisition.

His southern temperament, however, did not stop to bring him into a difficult situation. After he had obtained the venia legendi from the Oxford University he started his lectures with a speech on the immortality of the soul and on Kopernik´s planetary system, which was still a whispered hypothesis, heretical to all churches, Anglican and Protestant included. Small wonder, therefore, that Bruno was lectured severely by the Rector. If we believe Bruno he flattened him thoroughly in this exchange but the universities of England were closed to him hence. He in turn referred to the Oxford University as the „widow of the noble sciences".

When his protector was recalled to France Bruno accompanied him back. He resumed his lectures at the Sorbonne, inciting instantly the hate of the Aristotelians, of course.

His peripatetic blood told him to try the Protestant universities in Germany. He succeeded to teach for two years at Luther´s alma mater in Wittenberg. We do not know but can only surmise that also this station was left by him with an éclat; at any rate he did not embrace Protestant theology. He must have been of some fame already, because Emperor Rudolph II. in Prague allowed him to teach at the Helmstedt university. Foreseeably so this worked only for a few months, whereafter he was expelled there by the Lutheran Consistorium. Bruno went to Frankfurt, then to Zurich, and back to Frankfurt in 1590/91, where he enjoyed a spell of quiet in order to rewrite and publish his works in Latin.

We are using the spell here in order to have a closer look into the philosopher´s brain. Fact is that this brilliant brain knew neither system nor order. Each of his numerous treatises, some of them with bombastic titles, is a happy mixture of profound thinking, hyperbole, frontal assaults on any who would not share his views, but also of a wit that Goldoni would have envied.

The foreground of his mental stage is governed by his despise for the clergy, the church organization and obscurantism. Compared to Voltaire who saw the same goals Bruno used an axe where Voltaire applied the far deadlier weapon of his witty rapier. The inquisition had Bruno already in her sights, long before she struck.

What we are distilling from Bruno´s oeuvre here is his stupendously modern theory on the world, the universe surrounding us and on the infinity which is enveloping anything (treatise „De l´ínfinito, universo e mondo", 1584). Neither earth nor sun are centers of the world. Beyond our world, so he wrote intuitively and without knowing a telescope, there are other worlds, and beyond these still others without beginning or end. The so-called „fixed" stars are not fixed at all, as Kopernik thought them to be, but are also moving (the „fixed star parallaxis" of 0,3 arc seconds which proves their motion was measured only in 1839).

Since everything above our heads is in motion, so Bruno followed, this universe knows no center, no boundaries, no ups and downs. Moreover, since movement is measured in time, to relative motions there must be a relative time, preempting Einstein by 331 years. In all probability many stars must be populated by intelligent beings. To each population therefore, the revelation of God must come, through the one Christ or many Christs?

Since the cosmos is infinite also God must be infinite, or the other way round: God and the cosmos are one, therefore God is present also in the smallest parts of the cosmos called monades, thought to be smaller than Democrit´s atoms and carrying divine power. It was Bruno who transferred this concept from Lucretian to Leibniz. Visible nature is the „outside" of the all-pervading Divine Spirit. There is a principle of progress and change working in nature, every part of it strives towards further development; so Bruno was also preempting the concept of evolution.

Finally, we distill from his works, there are of course contradiction, counter-powers, contrasts in nature. Within the whole cosmos, however, this „iuxtapositio oppositorum" cancels each other out and vanishes, also the so-called Evil. We hear him speak: „Unity it is which enchants me. By her power I am free, yet in chains, happy in distress, rich in poverty, alive in death".

It was not given to this apostle of evolution to refine his incredibly modern ideas into a system that would work on for itself. We daresay that Giordano Bruno was drunk with God, struck with wonder and singing praise as only Italians can do it, passionate and enthralling.

He thought of returning to Italy but was not sure whether the inquisition had read all his works, especially the one with the title „Throwing out the triumphant beast", the synonym taken from the

Apocalypse and applied by him to the church. Fact was that he was already high on the list, declared on outlaw who should be grabbed at first opportunity.

Giovanni Mocenigo was a scion of an already old Venetian family who had supplied the Republic with a famous Doge already. Mocenigo dabbled in occultism but was a devout catholic. He had heard of Bruno´s memorizing technique and invited him to come to him as his teacher and guest. Bruno was only too happy to comply.

Things went not successfully between pupil and teacher, however. Mocenigo made only slow progress and surmised that his teacher would not initiate him fully into the art. Moreover he shuddered when he heard Bruno lashing out in his usual unstoppable Napolitano manner against the clergy and the church. In the confessional Mocenigo told his spiritual adviser of these horrible abuses and asked him whether he should inform the inquisition; the priest told him to pick a little more into the brain of Bruno. When Bruno however told Mocenigo that he planned to return to Frankfurt the trap sprang shut. On May 23rd 1592 Bruno was imprisoned by the Venetian inquisition. He should not see anything else thereafter than the squalor of dungeons, until his death.

Mocenigo, the eager informer of the inquisition, told them every „diabolic" detail of Bruno´s opinions: hostile to all religions, contesting the supernatural being of Christ and the Eucharist, saying that all monks are idiots who disgrace he earth, demanding that religion should be substituted by philosophy, holding fornication for a laudable institution - the list was long enough to last for ten instead of one accused.

From May to September 1592 Bruno was interrogated repeatedly. Preempting Galilei he recanted and asked for clemency. In February 1593 he was claimed by the Chief Tribunal of the inquisition in Rome. In order to break a man (or woman) the inquisition had not only the rack but a far more formidable weapon: time. Bruno reportedly was never tortured by mechanical means, but the intervals between one interrogation and the next were long and irregular, sometimes more than half a year. Repeatedly he complained about the food - without any reported redress. If we add darkness, isolation, cold, hardly a minimum of sanitation, rats - it is enough to break any body.

But not any spirit and not Bruno´s spirit. In December 1598 they gave him ink and paper for a full confession. On January 14th 1599 he was again interrogated, the accusation was that eight points from his books were heretical. He defended them but acknowledged that he would accept the Pope´s final decision on them. He did not have to wait long.

Already three weeks later Pope Clemens VIII. declared the parts in question as heretical. February, April, September and November saw again interrogations of Bruno. We may safely assume that Bruno knew that he would never be released and so he decided to take the initiative: on December 21st 1599 he declared that he would not recant anything. On January 20th 1600 he sent a letter to the Pope demonstrating that the indicted sentences were pried loose from their context. The Pope decided to make an end and asked the inquisition to have a last hearing on February 8th 1600. Bruno was defiant, feeling the end coming, to which he probably longed for as his redemption. The verdict was signed by nine cardinals, inclusively Bellarmin who should play the same infamous role in the process against Galilee later. The German convert Kaspar Scioppius was present when the verdict was read to Bruno, who told the judges calmly: „You may pass this verdict with greater fear than with which I receive it."

On February 19th they tied him naked to the stake that was erected in the Place of Flowers. They took care to gag his mouth so he would not have an opportunity to throw a last memorable sting into the crowd. So the man who had loved nothing more than talks and discussion died silently in the flames.

# THE DISCUSSION

W: Of all the historic figures whom we have invited to appear in our little book Giordano Bruno certainly is the most erratic person. To be „drunk with God" Novalis accorded to Spinoza much later but I feel that the expression befits Bruno much more.

B: Yes. Had he been a little less impulsive he could have stayed out of harm's way. But his Italian temperament always got the better of him; it steered him into final trouble.

W: Do you think that he would have avoided confrontation if he had sat down like a more northern philosopher would do, carefully honing his words and raising a tremendous edifice of faith?

B: In the end the outcome would have been the same, it only would have given him another 20 years or so. But I very much subscribe to the „edifice of faith", or philosophy, which he was apparently unable to errect. When speaking of God, his language becomes breathless and ecstatic. Could it be that this had an organic, physical reason within his body? He repeatedly admitted to have a voracious sexual appetite, so it could well be that his whole hormonal system was in disorder, maybe a thyroid hyperfunction included? This would explain the peripatetic behaviour and the erratic style of writing?

W: Unfortunately we have no painting of him so we cannot analyze ex post whether Bruno had Basedow eyes or not. It is also quite besides the point of our discussion, don't you think so?

B: No, I think that his physis and psyche are very much part of our discussion. I bet that in case some psychiatrists would analyze his prose they might come up with some not so agreeable symptoms he had, just as was the case with the analysis of Paul's syntax.

W: I could not care less, my friend. And do not forget that someday, perhaps, also our language could be under the microscope - what then?

B: As long as they feel that it was plain and yet not dull - they can think what they want to.

W: It is high time that we leave this point. Was Bruno a contributor to evolution?

B: Definitely yes. His visions of the infinite cosmos could not include a Big Bang as the cause thereof, but until Hubble detected the red shift of fleeing galaxies we had no proof of it either. Next, he did away with the Aristotelian notion of a „first unmoved mover" of matter. Bruno „saw" God manifested in all matter.

It is very intriguing to read a passage from the apocryphal texts that were not allowed in the church´s canon, where the Logos in Yeshua tells his disciples: „Split the wood and I am in there, break the stone - I am inside it". Bruno was feeling this very acutely also.

W: I admire the way he dealt with so-called Evil. He clearly saw Evil not as a necessary component of the creation nor as a fiendish cosmic assault on it, but as a de-railing of free will within reflexive creatures. Animals can do no Evil. If, Bruno reasoned, there are countless other intelligent habitats in the cosmos besides ours, this will require countless acts of revelation, because God is just. With each such revelation and in whatever form the good God tells his beings that he is, cares, loves. Much more love than Evil will be produced in the universe, therefore, and this love wins and will cancel out all population-made Evil from the creation in the end.

B: The revelation part of it we have called the spiritual cosmic principle in our first book, remember?

W: And how! We feel our opinions very much at home with Bruno´s.

B: Finally we have to give credit to Bruno for being the first to view time being relative to motion. I do not recall any statements in Einstein´s letters, treatises or in his biography (R.W. Clark) that he refers to the intuitive interpretation of Giordano Bruno?

W: It fails me also; if so, it certainly was not done on purpose. This would have been alien to Einstein.

B: Each time the ecstatic pendulum swung back within Bruno it touched the nerve of the present state of mind of the clergy, the monks, the church, the princes - and it made him wince.

W: If he had only winced, but he described this obscure corner of the creation in the same hyperbole as he had them in store for his praise for the wonders that God worked in the universe, only in reverse now.

B: Are you holding this against him? Is it not a contribution to evolution in your mind because he used outcries in both directions instead of constrained scholarism? We have seen an evolutionary bonus in any of the persons presented before him here, when they were attacking the fouling church system. So why not also Bruno, even when he was carried away constantly by his furor Italicus?

W: I apologize, you are correct.

B: The stamina of this man must be admired. To rot for 8 years in the prisons of the inquisition and still not ready to cave in - this is an outstanding achievement. I bow to it with all respect.

W: So do I. He could shoulder this, in my opinion, because he was the man he was. A scholarly man would have been broken within one year. A fiery mind like his developed inner barricades behind which he could retract until the next sadistic hearings.

B: So you wanted to say that it was his alleged hormonal imbalance which kept him fighting?

W: At least it contributed very much towards it.

B: Let me ask you very pointedly: what has Giordano Bruno contributed to the evolution of consciousness?

W: There is one answer only: he showed the world a far greater God than she ever had imagined - or would dare to. With that, any idea of a centrist role of our planet in the material or spiritual creation was absurd.

He was the first to assume the existence of other intelligent habitats in the universe. With revelations going on over our heads and under our feet in every moment we live, have done so prior to this earth´s existence, will go on long after our species has vanished - if this is not a reason to burst forth in a cry of utter wonder and joy - what else will do?

B: Quite so; and compared to this panorama you have these treacherous and corrupt priest churches on this world - it wants you to cry out again, but in utter despair now!

W: Of these two cries Bruno existed; I think he is heard today with much more impact than during his time.

B: What shall we write on his epitaph?

W: He wrote it himself: „De´l infinito, universo e mondo" - On infinity, the universe, the earth.

# BARUCH SPINOZA

## 1632 - 1677

# THE MAN

Baruch Spinoza was born in 1632 to a wealthy and respected Jewish family in Amsterdam. They came from a Jewish family in Espinoza in the Spanish province of León who had converted to Christianity, „conversos" as they were called officially, „marranes" - pigs - behind their backs. A probably non-converted part of the family emigrated in order to flee the inquisition, first to Portugal, then to France and finally settled in Amsterdam in 1593. Already in 1628 the grandfather of Baruch was recognized as the leader of the Sephardic community there, his father was elected many times as head of the Jewish school and president of the local synagogue´s welfare organization. Baruch´s mother died of tuberculosis when he was 6 years old.

His education began in good orthodox tradition in the synagogue school, centering on the Old Testament and the Talmud. He was not saying in his later years when he started to have the first doubts on the Scripture. As he grew up he must have heard of the great Jewish thinker Maimonides and his „Guide For The Perplexed" where he advocated allegoric interpretation of the Scripture in places where it confronted reason; Maimonides walked a narrow trail bordering on heresy in questioning the immortality of the individual.

We do not have his proof nor any other that the 15-year old boy witnessed the drama that enfolded his fellow Jew Uriel Acosta from 1618 until 1647. Baruch never touched the subject in his writings. Gabriel, who later changed his name into Uriel, Acosta came from a Portuguese converted Jewish family. Educated by the Jesuits in Portugal he felt sickened by their fire-and-brimstone theology; moreover he came to the conclusion that Christ had adopted Mosaic Law fully, which, therefore, should be accorded divine origin and not Christendom.

He persuaded his family to flee Portugal and the inquisition and to return to the old belief. They settled in Amsterdam in 1617.

The mind of Uriel was not to be satisfied by dogmas. Very soon however he saw that the Rabbinic dogmas tried to fence in his mind in the same way as the catholic ones. Moreover, he openly contradicted rules and rites which, in his opinion, had no basis in the Scripture. His first treatise „Protests Against Tradition" - meaning the Talmud - appeared in Portuguese language in 1616. He was unwise enough to forward a copy thereof to the Jewish community in Venice which, of course, banned him (1618). The Rabbis of Amsterdam, whom he had called Pharisees in the paper, demanded a recantation which Acosta rejected (1623). The five years´period between the two expulsions show that the Rabbinate in Amsterdam was hardly a fanatic or hasty organization.

In his next publication Acosta threw his gauntlet not only to Judaism but also in the face of christianism by denying the immortality of the soul. There is no proof nor justification of it in the Old Testament, he challenged. Now the Jewish community was fast to act, because they knew that if they were slow the uproar in the Christian camp could lead to hostilities and would endanger the religious freedom accorded in the Union of Utrecht 1579. So they informed the Magistrate of Amsterdam that Acosta was undermining christianity by his views. He was arrested, fined, and his book was publicly burned, but he received no bodily punishment and was released.

His younger brother who was dependent from him suffered far more under the ostracism that was imposed on them by the Jewish community. Maybe in order not to ruin his brother´s future, maybe because he wanted to marry, probably for both reasons, Uriel offered peace to the Rabbinate. His recantation was accepted (1633); he did not marry, however, which confirms the first reason of his withdrawal. His questioning mind, however, continued to work until the point where he discarded all religions and saw only a Divine Being identical with nature; with that he shoved the stepping stone under the feet of Spinoza by which this thinker could enter into the edifice of his later philosophy. At this time, however, young Baruch was still firmly siding with the orthodox community and, above all, his prominent family. Acosta was expulsed from the Jewish community again in 1639, surrounded by enemies, the most fervent one his brother.

For seven years Uriel Acosta could bear his fate as a non-person, but not any longer; he offered unconditional capitulation. The Rabbis imposed on him the theatre of Grand Penitence, taken from the Portuguese inquisition manual: to read his sins before the community in the synagogue and to swear to live within the faith and community ever after; to receive 39 whip strokes, half-naked, and to lie down on the synagogue´s doorstep where everyone stepped over him when leaving, his brother, not reconciled, as well.

When Uriel Acosta rose from the threshold his mind was firmly set on the next act. Back home he wrote his final reckoning with an encrusted Judaic faith „Exemplar humanae vitae" - example of a -his- human life, stating that all evil originates from not following reason or natural law. After finishing the manuscript he loaded two pistols, waiting for his brother to pass by under his window. He fired but missed him. The second shot was for himself.

Baruch Spinoza was 15 years old when he - probably - stepped over the prostrate and blood-stained Uriel Acosta. He may have closed his eyes to the sinner, but certainly not his mind.

How much Acosta contributed to the slow but steady defection of Baruch we do not know. He made the mistake, however, to discuss his doubts with friends who, in good inquisition style, first prompted him with leading questions and then informed the Rabbis.

The Rabbis had considered Baruch to be one of their most promising students and were, therefore, truly violated when Baruch fielded their inquest with the very opposite of the arguments they had fed him for years. It is reported but has never been verified that the Jewish leaders offered him an annual rent of thousand guilders if he promised not to question the Judaic (and Christian) teachings any more and if he would attend the synagogue now and then. If so, he refused.

They were very lenient to him in the beginning. The first punishment imposed on Baruch was not to have contact for 30 days with other community members. He reportedly accepted this with the comment „Well, I am not forced to do anything which I would not have done myself". Both sides knew inwardly that the final battle would not take long to come.

The patience of the Rabbis ran out in 1656. On July 27th the „Great Ban" on Baruch Spionza was declared in the Synagogue and before the secular authorities which were asked to ban him also from the city. The magistrate demonstrated more humanity than the priests and condemned Spionza „to some months" of exile, whereupon he moved to the near village of Ouderkerk. Within a short but not recorded time he was back to Amsterdam.

When his father had died in 1654 one daughter claimed the total estate for herself, calculating probably that Baruch in his semi-banned state would not dare to contest her. He did so before the secular court, however, won - and handed over the estate to her, minus a single bed. He earnt a small living with the grinding and polishing of optical lenses, especially for microscopes and telescopes. Huygens was praising the quality of his craft openly. He also taught Latin in a private school but all this added up only slightly above subsistence level. Spinoza was never poor, however, and it is reported that he dressed very carefully and enjoyed good food, wine, and the theatre.

The early death of his mother is an indication that the inclination for tuberculosis of the lung had been passed on to him. The microscopic dust flying away from the lens grinding found little resistance in him, therefore.

Since his excommunication he was known to the secular world as „Benedict" Spinoza, because Baruch in Hebrew language means „blessed". We prefer to call him simply by his family name here onwards.

Spinoza moved in a circle of scholars, led by Dr. Meyer and Simon de Vries. He was so well liked by de Vries that he wanted to bequeath his total estate upon his death to him. Spinoza however persuaded him to make de Vries'brother the universal heir. After de Vries'death this grateful brother offered Spinoza an annual rent of five hundred guilders; Spinoza finally consented to accept three hundred.

In 1660 Spinoza left Amsterdam because „the visits of his friends were not becoming his contemplations"; he moved to Rhijnsburg, near Leiden. Here, in a modest private quarter, he began the first book of his „Ethics" and finished a few minor treatises, e.g. the „Treatise on God, the man and his happiness" and the interesting paper „On The Improvement of The Intellect", all in Latin, of course, the lingua franca of all scholars up to Newton.

In these early writings only the contours of his image of God became visible. „The highest good" so he says in the „Improvement" is the recognition of unity which unites the spirit with all nature. And yet these treatises contain already Spinoza´s trend of argumentation fully. „I want to direct all sciences to one use and goal, namely to attain highest human perfection; so we shall discard anything in the sciences which does not further this goal." This is also the explanation why he gave the title „Ethics" to his most influential work.

He quickly made new friends in Rhijnsburg, especially the English Henry Oldenburg who in later years fell out with him when he had embraced the catholic faith and wanted to draw over Spinoza to his new belief.

During the Rhijnsburg years Spinoza wrote the first of his few books that were published during his life-time and it certainly was not one of his outstanding works, entitled „The Geometrical Proof of Descartes´ Philosophical Principles". It was an explanation of Descartes along the axiomatic reasoning of Euclid but bare of any additional gain of insight neither in his nor in Descartes´brain.

His unprinted opinions on religions, nature, God and the role of reason were already much more powerful than this one printed, dry book. So powerful that a Rhijnsburg friend of him, Adriaan Koerbagh, was put to trial in Amsterdam, accused of „boundless opposition againt the (Calvinist) confession". The source of his poisoning was seen in Spinoza; Koerbagh denied this but was sentenced to ten years in prison, where he died after fifteen months. Spinoza was not tried but knew that he was only an inch away from destruction. Thinking of Hus and Bruno he was in no hurry to have his works published.

In June 1663 he moved to Voorburg near Den Haag, ground lenses and wrote for six years, continuing his „Ethics" but finishing and publishing his famous „Tractatus theologico-politicus", the theological-political treatise. Why political?

In these years the fight between the calvinist clergy of Holland and the political leaders, the brothers de Witt, had reached a climax. The de Witts and their followers advocated freedom of thinking and, after having stayed off the rapacious incursion of their country by Louis XIV. and his field marshal Prince Condé, peace negotiations.

Spinoza was a staunch follower of this party, led by Jan de Witt. But instead of adding another ingredient to the boiling cauldron of church-state warfare his „Tractatus" spelled to the hotheads of either side measure, justice and fairness. On the title page he wrote the famous truth: „It is the intention to demonstrate that freedom for philosophy can be accorded without the least damage to piety or peace within the state and that this freedom can only be withdrawn together with piety and peace".

Spinoza was not rising as yet to the full height of his ideas as laid down later in the „Ethics". His treatise centered to unearth the human shortcomings in the Scriptures. „... and so I resolved to examine the Scriptures anew with unprejudiced and free reason and not to accept anything which could not be drawn from them in full clarity. Employing this caution I have adopted a method to interprete the holy books ...". We may rank Spinoza, and his Amsterdam friend Dr. Meyer, among the first eminent representatives of Higher Bible Criticism. It would lead too far in this abridged context to center on his skillful and devastating arguments in detail. Only that: the Bible is not the mastermind of natural sciences or philosophy. These are revealed to us by nature and this revelation is the most true and most universal communication coming from God ... The goal of philosophy is only truth, that of a religious belief however is only obedience and piety. The person of Christ made a deep impression on him. He discarded the notion of his bodily resurrection but conceded that he, and only he, had received a special revelation from God directly.

On the whole, however, this book was a declaration of war against the orthodox Judaic as well as christian church and was duly recognized as such. In June 1670 the calvinist church council protested to the Great Pensioner of Holland against this heretical danger. Likewise the rift of acclaimants and denouncers split through the whole civic establishment of the cities, especially in Amsterdam. To make it stick more easily in the minds of the uneducated they called Spinoza a Satan, atheist (which he never was), saboteur of veneration and religion, to mention only a few flatteries. Luckily for Spinoza the Great Pensioner Jan de Witt was still firmly in charge. Had Spinoza been a fiery iconoclast and igniting local uprisings then the secular authorities, even Jan de Witt, would have been compelled to step in. Spinoza however was a more wily demolitioner who was all the more devastating by his controlled rhethoric, intimate knowledge of the Hebrew language in the Scripts, precise piercing of issues and absence of abuse. Moreover, he wrote in Latin so his incendiary fell only into the studies of the scholars and the clergy. The orthodox Jews and Calvinists only bided their time.

Spinoza considered The Hague a more protective surrounding, so shortly after the appearing of the „Tractatus" he moved there, also nearer to the reigning Jan de Witt. In the house of Hendrik van der Spyck in the Pavillioensgracht he had a mansarde room and continued to grind lenses. He could not complain of solitude, though; he had many visitors and paid visits to influential persons, discussing with them also matters of state.

When the mob murdered the brothers de Witt in the streets of The Hague (Aug. 20th 1672) Spinoza wanted to run outside and call them murderers to their face, but his prudent landlord locked the door. The state power went to Prince William Henry of Orange who knew that he could reign only with the support of the calvinist clergy. After one reprint of the „Tractatus" in 1674, therefore, a decree went out to banish the sale of the book, to be followed by a resolution of the calvinist consistorium in 1675 to bring the attempt for any printing of Spinoza´s works to the immediate attention of the authorities. Between 1656 until 1680 there were about fifty warnings by the church bodies against the sale and reading of Spinoza. We may not be far off to surmise that Spinoza could not have had a better marketing support.

We are covering his life to the end and then will turn to his glorious „Ethics".

In 1673 Spinoza was offered a full professorship at the university of Heidelberg, which he politely declined. Good for him because the city, as the whole of the Palatinate, was devastated in the Restitution Wars, better called Devastation Wars, which the central power of Louis XIV. leveled against the disorganized German princely states. Surviving peasants in the Palatinate called their dogs „Turenne" for decades in memory of his willing executioner.

Spinoza was drawn into the fight of the war/peace factions at home by a folly of his own, innocent in his opinion but welcome munition to his enemies. Condé had marshaled the occupation of the Netherlands, against which the Dutch drew their ultimate weapon, the opening of the flood gates. During this stalemate an invitation from Condé reached Spinoza to visit him in his Utrecht camp. Spinoza consulted his Dutch authorities who might have seen in him a welcome negotiator for a much-needed truce. Both sides granted a safe-conduct to him and so he went. In hindsight it was naive of the Dutch leaders to expect that Condé, not to speak of the French king, would listen to ouvertures of peace - of all people - by a highly controversial philosopher. Condé was ordered away from Utrecht, so Spinoza missed him, inspite of waiting for some weeks there. Upon his return to Den Hague he was immediately threatened by a mob who wanted to „lynch the traitor". He wanted to talk to the riotous heap, but again his prudent landlord locked the front door.

Over all political turmoil his fame spread over the whole of Europe. He corresponded with many of the shining minds of his epoch e.g. Leibniz, while still pushing forward his monumental „Ethics". In 1675 he undertook to have the book printed in Amsterdam, but did not foresee the immediate polemics which became rampant. As he writes to Oldenburg: „... that there is a book of mine in print which tries to prove that God does not exist ... therefore some theologians indicted me before the Prince and authorities ... so I decided to postpone the publication ..."

In February 1677 his physician Dr. Schuller wrote to Leibniz: „I am afraid that Mr. Benedictus Spinoza will leave us soon; his emaciation seems to get daily worse". He was right - and by chance the only one to be with Spinoza during his last hour. He told Schuller his last will, how to settle his debts by the sale of his modest assets, and ordering that all manuscripts which he had not burnt should be published anonymously. He refused any church rites and died peacefully on February 20th 1677. He was buried in the graveyard of the New Church in The Hague. His manuscripts, especially the „Ethics" were edited by Meyer and Schuller within the same year in Amsterdam.

It is high time now that we are centering on Spinoza´s „Ethics". The full title „Ethica ordine geometrico demonstrata" - Ethics demonstrated according to the geometrical method" - is fearsome enough. His model was Euklid; he wanted to build one logical proof upon the other so that each resulting axiom would be the infallible basis for the next. He intuitively knew, however, that this high ideal could not be followed through but he felt that a geometric pattern would contribute to clarity, keep „affectations" out (as he called the perception through the senses) and, finally, would preclude the camouflaging of sophism by empty eloquence. In short, he went about to inquire into the behaviour of man and into the nature of God as objectively and serenely as if they were circles, triangles or quadrangles.

Forbidding as this seems to us it was all the more aggravated by the definitions he drew from scholastic thinking. His definition of „substance" is only more complicated when reading Heidegger.

Reality is the joining of matter and spirit, substance is reality. Only our senses force us to register this reality in the separate form of matter and spirit. And here Spinoza comes to one of the most meaningful sentences of his philosophy in saying that „... all things are animated also by the Spirit, if only in different degrees (omnia quodammodo animata)".

And now Spinoza rises to his full philosophical height: „God and substance are identical". God is not identical with matter nor with spirit, but he is the underlying reality and connection of both (Deus sive substantia sive natura) and, finally: God is the entity of all being.

God is not a person, but the sum of all spiritual and material existence, he said, and: human consciousness is but a part of the limitless, all-pervading reason.

In hindsight we clearly see why Spinoza was labeled an „Atheist" by the ignoramuses of his time. He robbed both the Judaic and christian faith of the eternal patriarch figure who, on one side, ruled the heavens but on the other was prone to human behaviour which was painted on and feared from him. Without Jahve, no God.

Spinoza went on without mercy: there are no miracles, because the will of God and the inexorable order of nature are one. Any disturbance in the connection of natural causes would be an intrinsic negation.

Man is but a part of the universe, and nature is completely neutral to him, as to any other being. One should not use for God or for nature the expressions „good, bad, beautiful, repulsive" because these are words which express individual sensory thinking like „hot" or „cold". And: Beauty is not a propensity of the viewed object but an effect (affectation) in the beholder. There is universal order in the fact that all things are part of one system of natural laws; within this order a cyclone is as natural as the splendour of a sunset. He recognized this universal system as the ever enduring revelation of the Divine Spirit, surpassing any noble and beautifully written book (he did not mention it, but clearly the Old And New Testament was meant, inclusively the Koran).

He was struck indeed by the universal order in nature, almost inebriated, as his contemporaries lauded him with awed respect. Novalis put it more bluntly: drunk with God he is!

When Spinoza dealt with the concept of a soul he ran into conceptual difficulties and fled for an instance into ringing sophism: „The soul is the body as felt from the inside; the body is the soul seen from the outside". He wanted to express the unity of body and soul, one substance again, only perceived in different form. „Nothing happens in the body without a parallel perception by the soul" - and vice versa.

We, in retrospect, cannot agree to this metaphysical notion. Due to the state of sciences at his time Spinoza could have no idea of the chemical, electrical, hormonal governance of our body nor of the composition of our brain layers with their stone-age heritage. That is: we are not at any given moment masters of our body nor of our consciousness, or of both.

He went on to be unkind to the soul: as far as the soul was the partner of the body in ideas, concepts, experiences and remembrancies it dies when the body dies. Only the part of the soul which is formed by the acceptance of the universal, natural system of nature, as she has seen the things in God - this part of her will survive in the Divine Spirit forever. Spinoza will not have known Buddhism very well. This notion, however, brings him into close relationship with the nirvana, the melting of the person-less soul into a person-less universal Spirit.

To another idea we feel more attracted, probably. Spinoza scolded the christian faith to consider this side of life to be a valley of tears only and to consider death as the portal to heaven or hell. To think of death daily is an offence to life, he wrote, and: „A free man will think of less than death, and his wisdom is not to pore over death, but over life".

Another immortal phrase he coined when speaking of the things that we conceive to be true or real. If so, he said, we are experiencing them „sub quadam specie aeternitatis - under the aspect of eternity" and these ideas include the eternal and limitless being of God.

Since Spinoza declined to see God as a Divine Spirit who would be not able nor willing to respond to the love of man he made us shiver in this universe, and Yeshua told us differently. Spinoza, however, followed his heroic view and found that there can - and should - be an „amor intellectualis Dei" - which is the acceptance and adaptation of our ideas and behaviour of and on the nature of things and the order of the universe.

It is definitely arbitrary to end here abruptly the presentation of Spinoza´s „Ethics", but within this short book we have no chance to do otherwise. Spinoza´s method was deduction and he believed in the statics of his edifice as fervently as any philosopher before and after him. But he shared the conviction of the scholastics that the essence, the being and the doing of God could be understood by our three-dimensional human brain. In trying to do so he rose above all religions and denounced them as man-made and man-governed. His thoughts were flying into arcane realms that before him no man had noticed nor entered. His success in the centuries thereafter was certain, where the church organizations lost the help of their secular arms - finally.

The pantheistic identification of Nature and God had its inevitable impact on the romantic movement that sprang up in Germany.

Herder saw the unification of religion and philosophy in the „Ethics", and the book did not fail to make its impression on Goethe.

The French embraced him as another representative of „clarté" but the British woke up to him only since the middle of the 19th century. Until then he was dismissed by a miffed Anglican Church as „this notorious heretic".

Over all differing opinions on Spinoza one thing must be upheld: Here was a man who lived his philosophy, the unity of man and work prevailed at all times. His early death at the age of 45 years may have been a blessing in disguise. Upon departing from this world he left curriculum and work shining over time. If he had still written at the age of 80 he might have become more harder, more dogmatist, more unforgiving? And nothing is more disturbing than a vision where Spinoza would have sobered of God.

# THE DISCUSSION

B: Spinoza accomplished what no other heretic before him could accomplish: he alienated the Jews, the Christians and the heretics of either side. Was he a super-heretic?

W: He had not the least intention to and would have been very angry if somebody had dared to call him that.

B: I think that basically he was a pagan, in the best style of Marc Aurel.

W: And of Julian?

B: Certainly not. Julian needed too much self-restraint in order not to lash out against the christian creed. Spinoza managed to puncture the Hebrew and christian organization with cool, almost scientific detachment, not once with an outbreak of passion, abuse or damnation.

W: That was the catchword - scientific. Did he really believe he could analyze God or Nature to the last meaning, or universal will?

B: Slowly, friend. He was not out to analyze God and Nature but to synthesize them. This is the cantus firmus of his whole stupendous „Ethics"; there is no dualism between matter and spirit, they are one. There is no difference between God and Nature because all things in the universe are also animated, in a form which our intellect cannot comprehend, but there is no „dead" matter.

W: Sorry, I cannot reconcile to his deterministic approach. Also Spinoza succumbed to the dangerous ideas of the scholastics that God, being, nature, acts could be explained rationally by our supply of human reason. And yet he went about his task in the „Ethics" like a teacher of geometry, from one apparent axiom to the next apparent deduction. Trouble is that they were infallible axioms only to him, and, one thing more: if only one failed then all others would be struck flat in the ensuing domino effect.

B: He was not only aware of that but based his whole reasoning on the progressive deductions. In other words, he didn´t see the procedure as a risk but felt it was the only way that our limits of perception could be widened. For him, the procedure was a great inner reward, the logic of it perfect. As to the determinism which you dislike: at his time this was the major breakthrough since Ptolimee; a universe that knows no center, least of all our planet; the motions of planets were calculable since Kepler. It is a great pity that Newton´s „Principia" appeared after Spinoza´s death only. But also without anticipating them he described a universe of beautiful order; since this order could be understood by humans beings that had the „intellectual love for God" the universe was also predictable in its existence, eternal, that is.

W: I feel that we could discuss the „Ethics" for weeks, but we have a task to do. Our question is again: „Did Spinoza contribute to the evolution of consciousness?"

B: I could not think of a philosopher who contributed more towards it. With me he ranks equally with Kant in the front row.

W: We must not only state it, but show it. So?

B: First I want to point to something which is evolutionary because he did not do it, namely to attack the faith organizations, be they Hebrew or Christian, because of their obscurantism, intransigence and disdain for the individual. Especially the Calvinist belief with its insulting concept of pre-determination offered itself to it.

W: Spinoza was a philosopher but also a realist. For him the no. One requirement was to stay alive, to be able to write, not to be buried in a dungeon. Jan de Witt had difficulty enough to keep him from the fangs of the Consistorium. Had Spinoza lambasted the organization also this John of Gaunt would have been helpless. We may be sure however, that de Witt and Spinoza´s friends tried to restrain him on this issue, successfully so.

It meant much more to Spinoza to lead a withdrawn life and to be able to go on thinking, writing, and - in his opinion - proving

(W): the grandiose vista that opens to a mind who determines to see God and Nature united, not exchangeable but as one being. Of this wine he was really drunk but sober enough to write about it in austere and serene prose.

B: He felt that every reader should feel this joy also; to be alive not by necessity but, since you exist by chance, you might as well enjoy it - feel joy and do right, as he said. In this he holds the mirror before the faces of the Old Testament prophets, of Paul´s and Augustine´s. Others whom we have presented in this little book did this also. He was the first, however, who told everybody that in order to enjoy yourself in God you can do so not only without a faith organization but also without scriptures and tradition.

W: This is precisely why both sides anathemized him.

B: I only feel that his notion of the soul is not so very evolutionary, or perhaps too far out at evolution´s universal end. According to Spinoza our soul, we prefer to say individual consciousness, is formed of two layers. The basic layer connects with the body, they form an entity. When the body dies, also this layer dies, meaning the extinction of personal consciousness and above all the absence of an ultimate dimension where this individual might find a perpetual existence, remembering who and where he was.

Spinoza saw no need for this; something like this could not be attained by faith nor works nor predestination, simply because it is superfluous and unimportant in the context of God and Nature. The other layer, however, which he labels as the intellectual love of God, parts from the dead body and unites with God/Nature forever, but without terrestrial remembrance.

B: As we have said in the foregoing presentation of him, this is pure Buddhism. Did he know Buddha´s teachings?

W: It seems so. In his riposte letter to Albert Burgh, a son of his friend, who had converted to Catholicism he told him: „Is it that you have examined all religions, the old and new ones, which are taught here and in India and on the whole earth?..."

B: But nowhere in his works he is making a short reference to Buddha.

W: That as may be. We proceed: has anything else furthered the evolution of consciousness in his works?

B: Oh yes, on an altogether different level now, that of the relations between state and church. The state, he said, has the right to enforce secular laws because they guarantee social life. Not so with religion. „Simplicity and probity of mind cannot enter man neither by the rule of law nor by any public authority, just as virtually nobody can be forced by power or by law to reach beatitude ... The right and highest authority to pass judgement on religion and to interprete it is the individual".

W: Did the State at his time follow this warning, or the orthodox beliefs?

B: Of course not. The State needed the support of the Calvinist church and the obedient silence - and money - of the Jewish community for his political goals, they in turn needed protection - voila!

W: Again something very un-evolutionary crosses my mind. The devastating criticism which Spinoza leveled on the synagogues did not preclude him from supporting the idea of the restitution of the Jewish state saying „... I go so far to believe ... that they will newly erect their state and that God will choose them a second time".

B: Well, for the first part he was truly prophetic in this. Why is it un-evolutionary?

W: Because he infers that they were the chosen people, and could become so again. I wonder how he could uphold this idea because on the other hand he disputed any direct revelation from God to the prophets of his people.

B: I am also a bit perplexed here, I must admit. But very evolutionary in my opinion he becomes when thinking and speaking about Yeshua, whom he also called „Christ". He accorded him the voice of God, made no difference between the man and the Logos in him, however. He only stated „... I

(B): have to admit that I neither confirm nor deny the teachings of certain churches on Christ because I openly admit that I do not understand them ... Christ has communicated with God in the Spirit". And now comes the heavy calibre which is also directed at Mohammad: „ I maintain, therefore, that nobody except Christ has received a revelation from God without having added his personal fantasies, nor in words nor in visions".

W: The muslimin will not like this at all, nor the Jews, because he ruled out the divine inspiration of Moses also.

B: It is too late for a fatwah against him. Spinoza is dead since more than 300 years.

W: I should like to put a few sentences of Spinoza at the end of our discussion. Taken from his „Ethics" they could have come as well from the four reports on Yeshua:

„Who has recognized correctly that anything follows from the necessity of the divine Nature and happens according to the eternal laws and rules of nature, he will find nothing worthy of hate, ridicule or condescension, ... a righteous man hates nobody, is irate at nobody, does not envy anybody, holds nobody in contempt, underestimates nobody and is in no way haughty ... he who answers insults by hate and tries to avenge them leads a miserable life ... hate is compounded by counter-hate but can be levelled by love ..."

Evolutionary enough?

B: Quite so, because Spinoza not only wrote this, but lived it.

W: Are we having a word for his epitaph?

B: There is no need to. He wrote it already: „Deus sive substantia sive natura".

# TRIBUTE
## TO THE GREAT ISLAMIC
## „HERETIC" OF THE FUTURE

# TRIBUTE TO THE GREAT ISLAMIC „HERETIC"
# OF THE FUTURE

W: Loyal to our intentions in the introduction we have combed history for an outstanding Islamic heretic - but found none. Is this now a comforting signal or an ominous one?

B: The explanation is that in the absence of a priest church and their dogmas Islam allowed a far greater leeway to philosophers than the European churches. Heresy could be committed practically only against a few basic tenets of faith, among them the divine revelation of the Koran and that Mohammed is a God-ordained prophet. Nobody in the centuries since the Hejjrah found a reason to question these.

With the Enlightenment of the 18th century in Europe, however, and the onset of Higher Bible Criticism, plus the achievements of the natural sciences the letter of the Koran collided with experience and reason. Has the world now to correspond to the Koran or can the message therein be interpreted to conform to our state of worldwide collective consciousness?

So, no reformers were needed in the past and we take that as a good sign for the tolerance of Islam, something that has been lately if grudgingly acknowledged by the other great religions. But now the time has come to question some basic tenets - and quite understandably there is nobody in sight yet to do so, an ominous sign indeed.

W: First you have to define just what would be a „great Islamic heretic"?

B: „Greatness" would be called for, bravery even, to speak out against the fanatic fundamentalists who want to rule the world by the letter of the Koran.

W: Like the Taliban in Afghanistan?

B: Or elsewhere. They see a world that has lost its „ethics", if it ever had one, and in many cases they are right: exploitation of

(B): the natural resources which benefits only the rich few, up to half of the youth unemployed in some countries and prone to rioting, therefore, no more unobtrusive help to the poor via the Zakat - Poor Tax -, but corrupted state welfare systems and a general loss of values that stabilized social life -

W: - with the exception of women, in all past centuries of Islam.

B: I agree that Islam holds a good many stone-age ideas that call for one or more brave men - and women, yes - to transfer many tenets to their mental museum, perhaps not as many as the Judaeo-Christian religion. Remember what we said about a new perspective in our first book? Also the stage of Islam is beset by many awkward torsos that are blocking the perspective. I doubt whether Islam will find the equanimity of mind to deal with these obstacles methodically and peacefully.

W: So far I have heard basically critical voices only from Madame Tamila Nasreen, Bangla Desh, who is not only calling for more liberty to Islamic women but is also questioning the purely litteral interpretation of the Koran.

B: A brave muslim indeed. But in front of the fanaticism she is exposed to she is living on borrowed time, alas. Moreover, for the same reason why Yeshua had to be a male, her voice will not carry far because she is a woman surrounded by a patriarchal ambiente. No, the great Islamic thinker must be a man, I am sorry, if he should have impact, and he must be an internationally known scholar. Only if a man of his calibre will turn round and tell the Muslimin that the Koran can indeed be interpreted as and when it contradicts reason. He has to be a man of superior standing because only he will rally followers around him that are of the same rank as he - and he has to convince at least one islamic government, feudal or democratic.

Somebody as Mr. Abdolkarim Sorusch of Iran, for instance, whom they call today already the „Luther of Islam". His ideas are running into the - justified - direction of the separation of state and religion. We shall see with great apprehension whether he will survive.

W: One thing is quite obvious, if I follow your train of thought: the uneducated young, the poor and those wielding secular power will be up in arms against him. The young proletariate because he seems to smash the last life boat, the return to the roots. The poor because they see little nutritional value in an allegoric interpretation of the Koran whereas the Mullahs provide them at least with the certaincy of heaven. Those who are holding secular power, be they feudal or elected governments have the most to loose over massacres that would not wait for long, quite possibly also a Jihad - Holy War.

B: This would mean that our great Islamic heretic would have to be a militant leader also?

W: Or must have one to rally to his side, I am afraid. Pure logic, Higher Koran Criticism, reformation of the belief - this will not come to the Muslim world peacefully from the pulpits, because already the smallest attempt to divest the Koran of its eternal infallibility would call for a fatwah, to be answered by a counter-fatwah. According to what we know of the onset of chaos today the strange attractors will take over - and no way backwards.

B: So you think that once heresy - we say „aggiornamento" - raises her head in Islam that there will be instant warfare among the factions?

W: Yes, and with everything they have; chemical, bacterial, nuclear.

B: Why are you so sure of that? UN-mediation will be ruled out, of course, because each fighting side will claim reasons of faith which are not subject to a vote in the UN. But the Arab League, for instance?

W: The League will rip through in the middle.

B: So the only chance to prevent disaster is for the non-muslim nations to act sooner than any of the holy warriors, telling them that the first shot at each other would trigger immediate retaliation?

W: I do not think that we should develop war games here. What we wanted to drive home is the point that reform in Islam will not happen peacefully and that our „Great Heretic" will act in constant peril of life, and not very long, probably.

B:  If you look back on the time of Luther and thereafter, would you call this a peaceful reformation?

W:  It is not comparable to the Muslim world of today. The wars after Luther´s reformation were waged for very secular motives, inclusively by the Roman and national churches. When Islam breaks apart in a „reason versus letter" war, it will be a purely ideological war, and all the more vicious so.

B:  So what is our tribute to the Islamic scholar of fame who dares to be the first heretic?

W:  We know that you will step forward, sooner or later, and we admire your courage. Bring your family to safety before you speak out because you know that your enemies will not stop at anything. Make sure that at least one prince, king or government shields you; you have to convince them before the masses.

    We fervently hope that war can be avoided; the chances are slim. One day, and this you also know, your murderer will strike, he cannot be stopped. And in this last moment, great man, we wish you the serene satisfaction that also you worked for a greater God - as your fellow „heretics" in this book did. Be in God´s glory! We shall meet.

# E P I L O G

## TOWARDS THE CHAOS OF UNDERSTANDING

W: With all due respect to the eminent men we have presented it must be said that the faith organizations against which they lashed out still exist today, together with their canonized creeds. Of course they are suffering from asphyxiation but it will take centuries of agony. Sudden death is nowhere in sight. Have our heretics suffered in vain?

B: Your old trouble is that you are viewing evolution always under the short-term angle. There is no such angle, only the far-out view to the horizon of our consciousness. A few terrestrial centuries are but some grains in the sand-clock of evolution.

W: This is the serene view which befits philosophers very well! But to hell, I say, I want to see at least some intermediate results also! Evolution is not snapping from one plateau to the next, it is slowly lifting our consciousness. But then, at some points in between, there must be some short tremor in the system indicating that an important barrier has crumbled, no?

B: In my opinion the past three hundred years have been tremor years only, politically, economically, especially so in the natural sciences. In the social and religious systems the trembling was felt also acutely and it led to some upheavals that, however, were far from the evolutionary arrow. The tremors there will go on far more rapidly there in the next hundred years, I am sure.

W: And where does all this leave our heretics? Could it be that they were too tame, centering on secondary values instead of proclaiming Holy War?

B: I do not like your term „secondary values". What do you mean by that?

W: Anything that comes after the primary values which are, in our opinion: God is, God cares, God gives, God wants. Anything beyond are „How To?" values, developed and rammed through by the faith organizations. On this level our heretics gave battle, sometimes magnificently so, but what about the primary values?

B: Not so, my friend. In your way of thinking this sounds as if our heretics had started a heated fight over recipés with other cooks in the kitchen without noticing that the food was poisoned and the kitchen walls crumbling. You are inferring that they did not dig deeply enough, down to the primary values, the kitchen fundaments. Well, not all of them did. But if you think of Luther and Spinoza, then the first certainly did not stop at the secondary tier where everything started but went down to rock bottom in positioning man/woman and their free will over organizations and dogmas; Spinoza had started with the primary values all along and was not going to be sidetracked ever after.

W: I do not think that I have made my point clear yet. In my opinion 99 per cent of the friction among the major creeds and sects of this world arises from the „How To?" differences, not so much from the four primary values, as seen by us. Well, the majority of the sects were born after our heretics. But, and this is my point: if the heretics had been more fighters than philosophers this probably would not have happened.

B: Suppose for a moment you were right. Where should the power come from to forestall these developments? There are only two possibilities, one of which is my old favourite. But let us start with the negative scenario: suppose the heretics had won, hands down, no more ecclesiastical nor secular opposition any more. Comparatively speaking the victorious heretic would have plenipotence like the Pope he dismantled. Would he not have used this singular opportunity to establish his edifice of faith? Perhaps not as a compulsory or state religion but as a preferred one nevertheless, preference coming from a benevolent secular government. How long do you think would

(B): this building hold? Not three generations, in my opinion. History would repeat itself very quickly: Dissident movements in the faith, a fat organization with the onset of arteriosclerosis, some dogmas perhaps to curb the most vociferous critics? And then: the new heretics are standing up - tutti da capo!

W: And your pet theory?

B: The positive scenario is that the heretics win also, have won already. Only: there will be no new organization, least of all a church. Instead there will be the global community of men and women of free will who connect to the four basic values as revealed through Yeshua: God is, God cares, God gives, God wants. And all the „How To?" will stay in their cultural tradition, peacefully side by side with all others.

W: I know your theory of a beneficial chaos period. But isn´t there the danger that a new order will form someday in this cauldron of beliefs, an order that would sweep minority beliefs to the sidelines, if nothing worse?

B: Not if the four basic principles are upheld. I think that the global community will watch over them pretty carefully.

W: And what about the heretics of this era?

B: In the „How To?" field there will be a discussion that will go on for some centuries. It is almost necessary that the secondary values are discussed, compared, split, united - what do I know. A multi-cultural „How To?" is far more preferable than a uniform code of veneration, as we see today.

W: And what about the rock bottom heretics, those who assail the basic principles?

B: As long as they speak as philosophers, they are welcome. This beneficial chaos in fact needs agnostics and atheists in order to become a boiling cauldron.

W: So another caravan, other barking dogs?

B: The comparison ends here, because a caravan is plodding on to a certain, known destination. My vision is the ever growing market place of human consciousness, extending in all directions.

W: You have not answered my question fully: What if the dissidents see that philosophy will not change anything and decide to preach revolution?

B: Then force has to be answered by more force, quite clearly. This global market place of which I am talking is certainly worth defending.

W: As a last word: what will be the main product of this market?

B: Evolution of consciousness.

---

# On the author

Widman was born in 1934 in Bavaria/Southern Germany. He entered the
[ban]king profession and was active in development banking, general
[cont]racting and export consulting for some 40 years.

[His p]rofessional life brought him into early contact with different cultures and
[relig]ions. This prompted him to take up the study of cultural history and
[philo]sophy since three decades, a never-ending and rewarding task in his
[opin]ion.

[Without] belonging to any church or sect he believes in a Creative Spirit which
[used] the man Yeshua as its intermittent mouthpiece. So-called christian
[chur]ches and sects made - and are still making - a singular travesty of this
[reve]lation. Evolution is not allowed to enter, so they end their life cycle as any
[prie]st-run organizations have done since 5.000 terrestrial years.

[Mr.] Widman's prime interest is to penetrate beyond their present burial
[plac]e. For him, evolution is a universal constant. This is why burnt-out faith
[orga]nizations, formerly criminal and corrupt, will sink into the abyss of
[obli]vion; not so the misused revelation, however. For her a massive
[evol]utionary metamorphosis is just coming up over the horizon, Mr. Widman
[main]tains.

[The] author is living in second marriage, has three grown children and four
[gran]dchildren and resides near Lake Chiemsee, Bavaria.

Books by Bert Widman :

# The Stone Age Of Faith

An evolutionary farewell
to churches and sects.
In plain language.
ISBN 3-89811-204-7

# Why, Paul ?

An evolutionary inquiry.
In plain language.
ISBN 3-89811-202-0

# Ahead Of Their Times

An evolutionary presentation
of eminent heretics.
In plain language.
ISBN 3-89811-203-9

GEORG LINGENBRINK GMBH & CO. PUBLISHER

Hamburg    Frankfurt